THE
Words
THAT
Inspired
THE DREAMS

THE Words THAT Inspired THE DREAMS

True Stories about the

POWER of a FEW CHOICE WORDS

CARON LOVELESS

HOWARD
PUBLISHING CO.

Our purpose at Howard Publishing is to:

- *Increase faith* in the hearts of growing Christians
- *Inspire holiness* in the lives of believers
- *Instill hope* in the hearts of struggling people everywhere
  ### Because He's coming again!

The Words That Inspired the Dreams © 2000 by Caron Loveless

All rights reserved. Printed in the United States of America

Published by Howard Publishing Co., Inc.,
3117 North 7th Street, West Monroe, Louisiana 71291-2227

00 01 02 03 04 05 06 07 08 09   10 9 8 7 6 5 4 3 2

Library of Congress Cataloging-in-Publication Data
Loveless, Caron, 1955-
    The words that inspired the dreams : true stories of the power of a few choice words / Caron Loveless.
      p. cm.
    Includes bibliographical references.
    ISBN 1-58229-124-1
      1. Encouragement—Religious aspects—Christianity. 2. Success—Religious aspects—Christianity. 3. Christian life. I. Title.
    BV4647.E53 L68 2000
    242—dc21   00-035052

Copyedited by Jennifer Stair
Interior design by Stephanie Denney

*For my priceless treasures
—Joshua, Jonathan, and Joseph—
who have filled me with endless delights
and made "It's a boy!"
three of the sweetest words I have ever heard*

*for my beautiful and talented daughter-in-love,
Rebecca*

*and for David,
the prince of my heart,
who said, "I do,"
and marked my life forever*

ABOUT THE AUTHOR

Caron Loveless is a gifted storyteller and passionate communicator. She is the author of *Hugs from Heaven: Embraced by the Savior* and the coauthor of *Hugs for Friends, Hugs for Teachers, God Things Come in Small Packages, God Things Come in Small Packages for Moms,* and *Taking Your Church off Pause.*

As a writer, pastor's wife, speaker, worship leader, and director of Creative Communications for Discovery Church, Caron is called upon each week to translate the life-changing truths of the Word of God in fresh and compelling ways.

A graduate of C.L.A.S.S. (Christian Leaders, Authors, and Speakers Seminar), Caron speaks at worship conferences, women's conferences, and retreats in the U.S. and Canada. She has been interviewed on *Life Today with James Robison* and was privileged to be a guest worship leader for a weekend service at Willow Creek Community Church in Chicago.

Caron and her husband, David, have been married for twenty-five years, and their three sons and daughter-in-law serve alongside them in various leadership capacities at Discovery Church in Orlando, Florida.

∾CONTENTS∾

FOREWORD

Some time ago I was attending the Sunday morning service of an old New England style church when the pastor spontaneously called on me to give the children's sermon. I had never given a children's sermon before and have not given one since, but because I had been invited there to teach the staff to become better speakers, I knew my credibility was at stake if I didn't come up with something fast.

Children streamed from the pews as I made my way to the front with no earthly idea what I was going to say to them. But heaven was one step ahead, for when I prayed, "Lord help me," I was immediately reminded of Ephesians 4:29, a verse my husband, Fred, and I had taught our own children, which says, "Let no corrupt communication proceed out of your mouth, but that which is good to the use of edifying, that it may minister grace unto the hearers" (KJV). Over the next few minutes, I enjoyed a spirited dialogue with my pint-size audience about the importance of our words, and God's command that we learn to speak only those that build and boost others, not cut them down or condemn them.

As I came to the last phrase in the verse that says our words should minister grace, I explained that when our words come out of our mouths, they should be like little presents all wrapped up to be given away. The children beamed at this idea—who doesn't love presents—and a few moments later I was touched as a precious little girl stood up, turned to the congregation, and in a loud voice proclaimed, "What she means is that our words should be like little silver boxes with bows on top." This was such a beautiful thought that it inspired me to write a book called *Silver Boxes*—a book on the value of verbal gifts of encouragement. And as a result, little silver gift boxes have become the shining symbol of my writing and speaking ministry.

Each year I meet thousands of people who hunger to hear one good word. That fact, coupled with my own personal experience, has fueled a passion to do all I can to give others hope through my words. The most significant moments in my life have been powered by words, so it is both exciting and fascinating for me to read the stories Caron has gathered here.

These stories, and the amazing people they represent, are proof of the power our words have to change lives. They are written in captivating, bite-sized portions perfect for our busy, read-a-few-pages, time-pressed lifestyles. Parents will want to share these stories with their children. Writers and speakers will want to take advantage of the valuable illustrations. Athletes and business and ministry leaders will be inspired by nearly fifty phenomenal success stories Caron has chosen to tell.

Whatever you do—prepare yourself. The words you are about to read could change your life.

FLORENCE LITTAUER

THANK-YOU NOTES

Thank you, John and Chrys Howard, Denny and Philis Boultinghouse, Ryan Howard, Gary Myers, and the incredible Howard Publishing staff. What a refreshing delight you are! The warm, humble, Christlike way you live your lives is the secret to your astounding success. I am honored to know and to work with you. Thanks for igniting my publishing dream!

Thank you, LeAnn Weiss, for your research assistance and constant encouragement. Your enthusiasm for this project and your support of our family through the years has been phenomenal.

Thank you, Leslie Aziz, Ralph Howe, Joanne Loveless, and Fred O'Neil, for your generous gifts of reading and research.

Thank you, Bernard Deloach, Nick Kroger, and Robin Ragsdale, for cheerfully plugging the holes I left at Discovery Church while finishing this manuscript. I couldn't have done it without you!

Thank you, Dr. Jack Groppell, Marita Littauer, and Pam Smith, for your kind and invaluable help securing interviews.

Thank you, Emilie Barnes, Dr. Kevin Leman, Florence Littauer, and Stan Smith, for graciously sharing your incredible stories with me and to all the others included in this book who kindly granted permission to tell their inspiring stories.

A huge truckload of thanks to my precious boys for fixing my computer problems, for "keeping it down out there," and for never complaining about the empty refrigerator.

And thank you, my "Captain O' Captain," for loving me unconditionally, being my loudest cheerleader, and proclaiming "Honey, this is really great stuff!" over everything I write.

MAY I HAVE A
WORD WITH YOU?

When I was in the sixth grade, our teacher gave the class an assignment to draw a palm tree. This was easy enough, since we lived in a state where palm trees grow like weeds. Happily, we scrounged around for colored pencils and busied ourselves with this task until, one by one, the teacher called us up to her desk to check our work. When my turn came, I presented my drawing and the teacher exclaimed, "This is a fine palm tree. I think it's the best in the class!" She may have added, "You're a genius! Perhaps we should send you to art school, contact the Louvre, and exempt you from math for the rest of your life," but it's been a few years, so that part's a little fuzzy.

As a result of this generous compliment, I was suddenly baptized with talent; and when school let out that year, I spent the entire summer sketching palm trees.

I was no child prodigy—maybe a notch above national average. But someone saw promise in me and said so—out loud. And every day since then I have believed without question that I am an artist.

In junior high, paisleys replaced palm trees, and I became school-famous for drawing the initials of my friends' romantic interests on their notebook covers. My sixth-grade teacher's words were with me there, as well as the times in high school when I reigned as "poster queen" for clubs, projects, and pep rallies. Later, her comments gave me the confidence to take design courses, throw pottery, start a ceramics business, sketch drama sets, make flower arrangements, study decorating, and paint a giant mural above my firstborn's crib.

I never became a great painter, but I did grow more creative. And now every day I am called on to dispense this creativity as a writer and as programming director at Discovery Church. At Discovery, it's my job to lead teams of artists, musicians, vocalists, actors, and technicians as they minister the spoken and visualized Word of God to thousands of people each year.

My teacher's words were short and sweet. It took little effort for her to say them. But they left a sizable mark on my life and ministry. She had no idea at the time, but for one brief moment, God borrowed her tongue, like Jesus once borrowed a donkey, to pick me up and cart me off toward my destiny.

You can probably think of a teacher, parent, or mentor who said similar words to you. Chances are he or she never knew the impact those words had on your life. And it is likely that, without even realizing it, your words have influenced someone else's life.

The Words That Inspired the Dreams is a celebration of life-giving words and the myriad ways God has used them over the centuries to call out greatness in the lives of his people. It is an eclectic collection of defining moments—some seemingly accidental, some born from the deliberate goodness or concern of another. The words were given to children, teenagers, adults, authors, athletes, ministers, business leaders, and others, spanning more than a thousand years. And in every case, the words that were spoken or written lived far beyond the one who received them.

As you read these stories, note the number of ordinary men and women God used to spark these memorable events. Most are people we would not spot in a crowd, folks who were minding their own business until God assigned them to his. They are all, almost without exception, ordinary people—mothers and fathers, welders and warriors, people from normal neighborhoods, mostly obscure, humblingly human—people like us.

A few years ago, I went to the mailbox and pulled out a copy of *Reader's Digest*. And as I flipped through the pages, the title of an article caught my eye: "Four Words That Changed a Life." The article was written by Bob Greene of *The Chicago Tribune* and recounted the story of Malcolm Dalkoff.

Malcolm was in high school when his English teacher, Mrs. Brauch, wrote a comment in the margin of his paper. The comment was almost too simple to be significant, but it rocked Malcolm's world. She wrote, "This is good writing." That's all. Before reading those words, Malcolm figured he was just an average writer. But that afternoon, he went home and wrote a short story. And thirty years later, he dropped back by to thank his teacher. Malcolm had become a professional writer, working mostly in advertising, and he wanted to thank Mrs. Brauch for the simple yet significant contribution she had made. He wanted her to know that he was now encouraging others to write. He just wanted to say that her four small words had made all the difference in his life.

And now her words are touching you. It was because of them that I decided to write this book.

It's true that actions sometimes speak louder than words. And yes, we are the sum total of *all* our yesterdays. But for most of us, there are a handful of yesterdays that loom taller and shine brighter than the rest, and they're usually marked by words.

If you get half as inspired reading these stories as I have been, it will be well worth the price of admission. I pray the moments captured here will enrich your life and heighten your personal influence. And, most of all, I pray that they dare you to make a difference with your words.

By the way, should you ever need a drawing of a palm tree, I know where you can get a really good one.

How good is a timely word!

—PROVERBS 15:23

1

CHOICE WORDS OF CHALLENGE

The 358-Million-Dollar Question

You never know when a moment and a few sincere words can have an impact on a life.

—ZIG ZIGLAR

She was just one woman trying to make a difference in her corner of the globe. Nothing particularly unusual stood out about her. When she walked down the street, no heads turned, and no one asked for her autograph. Certainly no one would have guessed that she would launch a worldwide movement.

Setting out from Grand Rapids, Michigan, Tena Hoelkeboer had trudged halfway around the world to the town of Amoy in order to teach Chinese girls. Every day, she and her four hundred students faced poverty, overcrowding, and malnourishment. Though her life was a struggle, Tena knew these children were her own private mission from God.

One day Tena met an American named Bob who happened to

be visiting a nearby university campus. Bob was traveling through Asia on a speaking tour for Youth for Christ, and as he stopped in different cities, he made a point to spend part of his time encouraging missionaries and taking pictures of their work.

Tena was delighted when Bob agreed to speak about God to the students in her school. But during his presentation, he used an American style of communicating the gospel of Christ. At the end of his talk, Bob invited the kids to receive Christ and said, "Go home and tell your folks you're going to be a Christian."

When Bob returned the next day, there was trouble. Tena met him at the door with a young girl dangling from her arms. The child's father had disowned her, and her back was bleeding from the beating he had given her when she announced her intention to live for the one true God. The father was enraged that his daughter had dishonored his ancestors by turning to Christ.

Tena's eyes blazed at Bob. She was incensed that his "American-style" altar call and cultural insensitivity had resulted in the beating and abandonment of yet another child. She walked over to him, put the girl in his arms, then said something that probably did more to save the lives of starving children around the world than anything else.

With tears streaming down her face, Tena said, "She listened to you. She believed what you told her, and she obeyed God. Now look what it's costing her! Don't think you can walk off this island without doing something for her. I've got six other little kids already sharing my rice bowl. Now you've given me one more. Tell me, what are you going to do about her?"[1]

That was it. Bob felt shaken to the core as he held the frightened child. He knew he didn't have the funds to save all the needy, deformed, and leprous children he had already seen on his trip. But he could rescue and support this one, whose name, he discovered, was Tam. Immediately, Bob dug in his pocket for money to feed and clothe the girl. And as he did, a vision was born.

That was 1947.

Within two years, Bob and Dr. Frank Phillips formed an organization to help missionaries meet the emergency needs of Korean War orphans. By 1961, they were supporting fourteen thousand children from 156 orphanages in nine nations. By 1998, their organization raised $358,351,000, sponsored 1,383,218 children, and met the spiritual, emotional, and physical needs of more than fifty million people.[2]

It was just an off-the-cuff remark. But God used an ordinary woman to speak to an American man about a homeless Chinese girl. Tena's challenge, delivered at a ripe moment to exactly the right person, made all the difference.

The man's name? Bob Pierce. His organization? World Vision—now the largest international Christian relief and development agency in the world.

YOU MIGHT LIKE TO KNOW

In 1967, Bob Pierce retired from World Vision due to illness. After a year in the hospital, he was offered the opportunity to lead another relief agency. You may have heard of it—Samaritan's Purse. The flyleaf of Bob's Bible contained this phrase: "Let my heart be broken with the things that break the heart of God." He died in 1978.

A Mere Suggestion Made the Difference

If people only knew how they might cheer some lonely heart or lift up some drooping spirit, or speak some word that shall be lasting in its effects for all coming time, they would be up and about it.

—DWIGHT L. MOODY

Chuck was in trouble. Big trouble. Just about the biggest kind of trouble a guy could get into. He had seen this kind of scenario before, and he was well acquainted with the possible outcomes. It didn't look good.

Chuck's was not the kind of problem you could handle by yourself in the privacy of your own home. It wasn't stretching things to say that just about the entire world had read something about his predicament. He was becoming famous, but his was the type of fame a guy could do without.

With the media hounding him, Chuck figured it was a good time to get out of town. But before he took off, he wanted to make one stop to see his longtime friend Tom. Maybe Tom could shed some light on the situation or offer a bit of advice.

Tom's wife greeted Chuck at the door, and the two men made their way out to the back porch. There wasn't much point in small talk, so Chuck got right down to business. He had seen a change in Tom's life, and now, with the courts breathing down his neck, Chuck suddenly wanted to know more about that change.

Tom began by relating the journey of his business success. He recounted the details of his rise to the presidency of the largest company in his state. In the eyes of the world, he had it all. But he didn't have everything. Tom knew he was missing something, but he wasn't exactly sure what.

Chuck listened attentively. He could relate to this feeling of emptiness.

Finally, Tom described a great spiritual discovery he had made one night in New York City. The discovery made him feel peaceful for the first time, and as Tom strolled the sidewalks in the dark, he said the lights of the city seemed to glow brighter and his fears began to fade.

Tom's discovery had been a personal relationship with Jesus Christ.

Chuck knew about God, but he never understood how a human being could experience him. Tom's story sounded nice, and his newfound faith was evidently working for him, but Chuck wasn't the religious type. He didn't want to do something drastic just because he was in hot water. As a marine, Chuck had seen several guys who turned to God in the trenches but went back to their old ways of life when they were out of their foxholes.

As the men talked, a book lay on the table next to them. At a certain point in their conversation, Tom picked up the book and made a suggestion. It was a natural suggestion, one that happens every day. It's the kind of suggestion you make to a friend and, sometimes, if you're eager, to a stranger. In the moment, you don't stop to wonder if your suggestion has eternal or international implications. You just make the suggestion because you feel led to make it. As it turns out, Tom's suggestion would impact thousands of people across the globe, a reality that neither he nor Chuck could imagine at the time.

Tom held up the book and said, "I suggest you take this with you and read it while you're on vacation. Let me read you one chapter."[3]

As Tom began to read, Chuck squirmed in his seat. Right away, the author seemed to put his finger on several wrong attitudes that Chuck had prized all his life. Some of these attitudes had been responsible for getting him into the deep trouble he was in. Chuck felt exposed. The words stung. He wanted to protest, to defend himself. Surely Tom understood there were legitimate reasons for his behavior. By the time Tom finished, Chuck was in agony.

Closing the book, Tom leaned forward and confronted Chuck about the issues in his life. Then he gently asked if he was ready to make the same step with Christ that had revolutionized his life. The book had been convicting, but Chuck wasn't convinced. He said no.

Then, before Chuck left, Tom took a minute to read a passage of Scripture and to pray for him. This hit an unexpected nerve. Walking to his car, Chuck was choked with emotion. And as he backed out of the driveway, he was sobbing so hard that he was forced to stop the car.

Over the next few days, Chuck took Tom up on his suggestion, and as he read the book, something happened. Chuck's fears, tensions, and animosities began to drain away. He came alive to spiritual things, and slowly, the void in his soul began to fill with God.

Chuck was still in trouble, but now, at least, he wasn't alone. His friend's simple challenge to read a book had led him to the Savior.

The book was *Mere Christianity* by C. S. Lewis. And the man who read it was Charles Colson, who at that time was special counsel to President Nixon. Colson later pled guilty to a charge of obstruction of justice in the Watergate scandal and served seven months in prison.

Today, thousands of people who find themselves in trouble look to Chuck Colson for help, hope, and guidance. Since reading *Mere Christianity*, Chuck has authored more than seventeen books of his own, the latest being *How Now Shall We Live?* His first book, *Born Again*, tells the story of the infamous back-porch meeting with his friend Tom Phillips. Chuck has become one of the most respected Christian leaders of this century. He is a leading spokesman for criminal-justice reform and is the founder of Prison Fellowship Ministries, one of the largest evangelical prison outreaches in the world.[4]

YOU MIGHT LIKE TO KNOW

Charles Colson was in church when he discovered the title for his first book. When it came time to sing, Chuck's wife, Patty, opened a hymnal and smiled. Printed at the top of the page was the name of the hymn, "Born Again." Other significant ministries launched by Chuck include Fellowship Communications, developed to produce publications to mobilize the Christian church for social action; Neighbors Who Care, to assist victims of crime; and Angel Tree, to provide for the needs of prisoners' children.

The Hero and the Schoolboy

How many people stop because so few say go.
—CHARLES SWINDOLL

The auditorium was packed. More than a thousand students crammed in to hear the speech by a national sports hero. As he walked to the front of the stage, the man put his hands in his pockets and let a deep silence fall on the room. Then, with a booming voice he said, "Do you know who you are? You don't, eh? Well, I'm here to tell you. You are Americans, and you are children of God. You can be somebody. You can be anything you want to be if you have a goal and will work and believe and have good moral character. You really can be what you want to be with the help of the good God."[5]

For a moment, the speech inspired the kids, but when the applause died down, the students all filed back to class and forgot about it—all except Jesse.

Throughout the talk, Jesse sat on the edge of his seat in the front row, his eyes fixed on the speaker. The hero had passion and had achieved something Jesse admired. Every word of the speech was etched in the young boy's mind—so firmly in fact that, even decades later, he could still recite it from memory.

That day as the auditorium emptied, Jesse hopped onto the platform to meet the speaker, and when they shook hands, the boy felt an impulse like an electric shock jolt through his body. At that moment, the torch was passed. And from that day, the path of Jesse's life lit up like an airport runway.

Throughout high school and college, he ran hundreds of miles as enthusiastic coaches helped hone his remarkable athletic ability. But Jesse's road was far from easy. Since they had six other children to clothe and feed, his parents couldn't afford to pay for his education. So in addition to classwork and a grueling training schedule, Jesse worked odd jobs before school or late at night.

Then, finally, on one of the most thrilling days in American sports history, the hero's words bore fruit, and all Jesse's work paid off.

The man at Jesse's school that day had been American track star Charlie Paddock, hailed on many sports pages as "the fastest human alive." And Charlie *was* the fastest, until 1936. That's when the boy in the front-row seat, Jesse Owens, astonished the world by returning home from the Olympic games wearing four gold medals.

YOU MIGHT LIKE TO KNOW

In his later years, Jesse Owens organized Junior Olympic games for eighteen hundred inner-city youngsters between the ages of twelve and seventeen. He also sponsored clinics with nationally known athletes as instructors. He said, "The top athletes can keep the kids interested and out of trouble. They inspire kids, just as I was inspired by athletes when I was younger."[6]

∞

The Challenge of a One-Minute Question

A man leaves all kinds of footprints when he walks through life.
Some you can see…others are invisible,
like the prints he leaves across other people's lives.

—MARGARET LEE RUNBECK

Ken was no stranger to church. From the time he was a baby, his parents had taken him to religious services. In fact, his middle name came from a Presbyterian minister. But this time, Ken and his wife had had it. After the ugly firing of their much-loved pastor, they thought, *If that's what church is all about, forget it.* And for the next fifteen years, their spiritual lives took a nosedive.

But while spiritual things took a backseat, Ken's career suddenly kicked into overdrive.

One night at a party, Ken met a man who was destined to

become his partner in one of the greatest achievements of his life. The man was working with a psychiatrist on a book called *One Minute Parenting*, and as the two men discussed the project, Ken explained that he had been teaching similar principles in the business world for years. The next week, the man, whose name was Spencer, sat through one of Ken's management seminars and became so fired up by the concepts that afterward he ran up to Ken and said, "Forget parenting! Let's go for managers."

It was then that Ken Blanchard and Spencer Johnson joined together to write a little book called *The One Minute Manager*.

Within a month, the men were handing out copies of the first draft. Five months later, the book was ready for sale to its first official audience at the National Restaurant Association Convention in Chicago, where a friend of Ken's arranged for a slot on the program. And just twenty minutes after Ken's presentation, *The One Minute Manager* sold its first thousand copies.

A year later, with very little promotion, the book had sold twenty thousand copies. Confident they had a good thing, Ken and Spencer decided it was time to put their book in the hands of an even wider audience. Along with their literary agent, Margaret McBride, Spencer pitched *The One Minute Manager* to a host of New York publishing houses. Many were eager to publish it. They signed with William Morrow.

The One Minute Manager became an overnight success! Only two weeks after publication, it hit the *New York Times* bestseller list and made its home there for the next three years.

Soon after the book took off, Ken got a call from his longtime friend and college buddy Phil Hodges. Phil worked in Los Angeles for the Xerox Corporation, where he was a top labor-relations officer. He told Ken that he just wanted to get together to catch up on things and suggested they meet for a walk on the beach at La Jolla.

As they walked, Phil posed a probing question. He asked, "Ken, why do you think *The One Minute Manager* is such a runaway bestseller? Is it that you're a better writer than anyone else or that you're smarter than most people?"

Ken said, "No, Hodge, I don't think that at all. I've thought a lot about it. I think the Lord wanted the book written, and he just used Spencer and me as his channels. When I go back and read the book, I can't even remember writing certain parts of it. The book seemed to write itself."

Ken believed in God, but when it came to Christianity, he had his doubts. However, Phil's words made him think long and hard about his spiritual condition.

Three years passed.

Then one day, while on his way to a speaking engagement, Ken ran into Bob Buford in the airport. Ken knew Bob was a Christian who ministered to business leaders and pastors of large churches. To Ken, it seemed providential when he discovered that the two of them would be seated across the aisle from one another on the flight.

By an interesting coincidence, Ken found a copy of Campus Crusade's *Four Spiritual Laws* booklet in his wallet that Phil Hodges had given him, but he hadn't remembered keeping it. A few minutes later, he leaned over and said, "Bob, this booklet is in my wallet for some reason. Maybe it means we should talk about Christianity. I have a few questions I'd like to ask you."

Bob Buford, and later, pastor Bill Hybels of Willow Creek

Community Church, thoroughly explained God's plan of salvation to Ken. Most of what they said made sense, and Ken carefully considered the claims of Christ. But he still wasn't ready to make a commitment.

Then in 1986, Ken experienced a gut-wrenching crisis. He was forced to consider drastic measures regarding his company's president and the future of their working relationship. For days Ken stewed in anguish, mulling over his options until, finally, he came face to face with his own glaring inability to find a solution. He knew he couldn't work things out alone. In desperation, he bowed his head and prayed, "Lord, I can't save myself here. I can't solve problems like this without your help. I admit I need you and recognize my vulnerability. I accept Jesus as my Savior and the bridge between you and me."[7]

As Ken prayed, a great peace came over him. For the first time, he felt the assurance and relief that God was present, guiding and directing his steps. Suddenly, regardless of the outcome of his company, Ken's new bottom line was this: With Christ in the lead of his life, he could manage anything.

It has been fifteen years since Dr. Ken Blanchard prayed that prayer. By now, *The One Minute Manager* has sold more than nine million copies and still remains on bestseller lists. It has been translated into more than twenty-five languages and is regarded as one of the most successful business books of all time.

Dr. Blanchard has gone on to author other books, including *The Power of Ethical Management* with Dr. Norman Vincent Peale, *Gung Ho!* with Sheldon Bowles, and *The Heart of a Leader* with Bill Hybels. In 1999, he coauthored *Leadership by the Book* with the two men who have been most instrumental in his spiritual life, Phil

Hodges and Bill Hybels. Dr. Blanchard is the chief spiritual officer of the Ken Blanchard Companies, a management training and consulting organization.

Concerning the talk on the beach that day, Ken said, "That meeting with Phil Hodges marked the renewal of my spiritual journey that had begun when I was a little guy being taken to church by my parents. Afterward, Phil kept calling me, sending me things to read, pushing me to think about my relationship with Christ."[8]

Ken Blanchard knows the power of a few choice words in a well-timed question, and he is living at a whole new level because of it. Who in your life could use a walk on the beach or a talk over lunch this week?

YOU MIGHT LIKE TO KNOW

After Ken's spiritual conversion, his wife, Marjorie, and both of their children also made decisions for Christ. Ken Blanchard and Phil Hodges founded the Center for Faith Walk in Leadership in an effort to assist leaders as they walk out their faith in the marketplace.

About the change in Ken's life, pastor Bill Hybels says, "The greatest change I've seen in Ken's life is a newfound exuberance in his work with marketplace executives. Instead of just challenging leaders to grow their organizations, now Ken is challenging leaders to grow their hearts and souls as well. Ken's faith is affecting everything he does and everyone he touches."[9]

A Party to God's Purposes

Say what you want to say when you have the feeling and the chance.
My deepest regrets are the things that I did not do,
the opportunities missed and the things unsaid.

—CAPTAIN JIM KELLER

The plans called for a cozy honeymoon, but instead of love and romance, the air was filled with strife. Apparently there were a few things that the groom had neglected to tell his young bride, so he sat her down to set her straight.

"Kay, now that you're my wife," Tom announced, "here are the things I don't like about you, and I want them changed."[10] Naturally, Tom's ill-timed comment and the listing of her flaws incensed and devastated Kay. An argument erupted, and in a matter of minutes, the honeymoon was history.

At the beginning of their relationship, Kay had been so drawn to Tom's creative, sensitive nature that she had failed to notice his dark side. But as their marriage progressed, it became obvious that Tom was an unhappy man. He tried switching careers, but nothing seemed to satisfy him, especially Kay. A few times he even threatened suicide.

But Kay's heart had grown cold and callous. After one of his threats, she mocked, "Do a good job so I can get your money!"

Sharp words and quick comebacks were Kay's weapons in her fights with Tom. One night, during a particularly heated exchange, she gave Tom such a tongue-lashing that he slapped her in the face.

"That's it!" Kay shouted. "It's over!"

Though Tom pleaded for another chance, Kay was finished. And when she went to her priests for support, not only were they in favor of separation, but one of them went so far as to put his arms around her, kiss her neck, and say, "You sure are a good-looking gal, Kay."[11]

With her two young sons in tow, Kay headed home to Virginia. Soon she and Tom were divorced.

Desperate for love and determined to get it, Kay went from one man to another. She spent two years in an illicit affair with a married man who was the father of six children. But inside Kay was miserable. She knew the life she was leading was wrong, but she always found ways to justify it. Eventually the affair ended, but Kay felt troubled, her heart held hostage by a number of flagrant sins. *God,* she thought, *if only I could have a fresh start!*

One evening, Kay sat talking with a friend at a party, and as she told the man her troubles, he looked at her and asked the question that would radically alter her life: He said, "Why don't you quit telling God what you want and tell him that Jesus Christ is all you need?"[12]

The man's comment felt like another slap in the face, but this time the words came from God. Their stinging power drove Kay to her knees.

The next morning, Kay notified her employer that she wouldn't be in for work. Then, by the side of her bed, she committed her life to Christ. "God, I don't care what you do to me," she prayed. "I don't even care if I never see another man as long as I live. I don't care if you paralyze me from the neck down. Just give me peace!"[13]

As Kay prayed, peace did come. Suddenly she felt clean and alive. And as the days passed, her need for a man was replaced by a ravenous hunger for God's Word. Reading the Bible made many things clearer to Kay, particularly her relationship with Tom. In time, she became convinced it was God's desire that she reconcile with her husband. But before she could make plans to see him, Kay received a phone call from Tom's father. Tom had hung himself.

Kay grieved Tom's death, and suddenly she was plagued with "what-if" questions: What if she'd acted faster? What if she'd met Christ sooner? Would Tom still be alive?

All through this sad, uncertain time, Kay sought solace in the Bible. She devoured large portions of Scripture, often driving with a Bible on her steering wheel. For the first time in her life, the Word of God made sense to her.

Before long, Kay's love for God and her zeal for his Word led her to attend a Bible college in Chattanooga, Tennessee, where she would lay the foundation for making one of the most significant contributions to the cause of Christ by a woman in the twentieth century.

The woman who went looking for love in all the wrong places is Kay Arthur, who over the past thirty years has pointed millions of people to the Master. She is known throughout the world as the executive vice president of Precept Ministries, which she cofounded with her husband, Jack, in an effort to help as many as possible learn the truths of God's Word for themselves. What began as a Bible study for teenagers has now exploded into thirty-five different Precept upon Precept Bible studies used in fifty states, 116 foreign countries, and available in fifty-four languages. Kay hosts three radio shows and has authored more than thirty-nine books with more than four million copies in print, including her latest, *Our Covenant God*. In 1998, nine thousand people attended more than one hundred regional institutes to learn her inductive method of Bible study or to be trained as a Precept Bible study leader.[14]

A "what-if" question we could ask is, What if Kay's friend at the party had kept silent? Would she still have found Christ? Would her ministry still have helped millions? Possibly. But one thing we do know for certain is this: On that night, and for his own sovereign purpose, God chose the powerful words of a friend to pierce Kay's heart and claim her for himself.

YOU MIGHT LIKE TO KNOW

Kay was twenty-nine years old when she gave her life to Christ. One day, she sensed God saying that she would indeed have another husband. "Well then, God," she said, "you pick him out and bring him to me!"[15] On a spring evening at Bible college, Kay and her boys were in the campus ice-cream shop when they spied a missionary to South America named Jack Arthur. Though they'd never met, Kay and her sons recognized Jack from his picture on their missionary prayer card. The four chatted briefly, and when Jack returned to Kay's school that fall, he called her for a date. Three months later, they were married.

A CHALLENGING WORD FROM GOD

Turning around, Jesus saw them following and asked,
"What do you want?"

—JOHN 1:38

Just as Christ did with the early disciples, he allows us to tag along behind him for a time, but sooner or later he will ask us to declare our intentions. He knows that sometimes we are fickle followers, our right hands reaching for the Bread of Life while our left hands grab for the cookie jar. And though Christ is infinitely patient with us, at some point will turn and ask us, "What do you want?"

Our problem is that we don't always know what we want. There are so many choices, so many options on the menu of life. But like a good father, God knows that all we'll ever get from riding the fence is splinters. So he shines his truth in the face of our ambiguity and prods us toward a decision.

When Jesus asked his disciples "What do you want?" they answered him with a question of their own: "Rabbi, where are you staying?" Jesus responded back with the words that would alter the entire course of history, words he still offers fresh to us every moment: "Come, and you will see."

At this moment, if Jesus suddenly turned and challenged you with the question "What do you want?" what would your answer be?

BOOST YOUR OWN WORD POWER

Become a missionary of encouragement. Challenge the dark-ness one soul at a time. Reject the mentality that says the needs in this world, my town, or my family are insurmountable. As you go about your day, focus on individuals. Use words to scatter hope!

Acquire a passion for great books. Keep a stack on your desk, beside your bed, and in your car. Give books as gifts. Tell people about the books that inspire you, especially ones that fan your flame for God.

My mouth will speak words of wisdom;
the utterance from my heart will give understanding.

—Psalm 49:3

2

CHOICE WORDS OF CALLING

Caught by the Substitute Preacher

Make the most of the present moment.
No occasion is unworthy of our best efforts. God often uses humble occasions
and little things to shape the course of a man's life.

—PRESIDENT JAMES GARFIELD

A blizzard was blowing through town, but the man buttoned his coat, slapped on a hat, and started for church anyway. Never mind the bitter cold and blinding snow. He was a longstanding member of the Primitive Methodist Church on Artillery Street, and each Sunday, no matter what, it was his task to light the stove and straighten the pews before the others arrived.

But that day, most of the congregation stayed home. By service time, little more than a dozen people had made it to church. Conditions were so bad that the pastor didn't even show up. Folks huddled together and looked around, wondering what to do. Maybe someone should pray or bring a word, but who?

The man volunteered. To the others, he was just a brother in the church who had little education and no theological training.

No one expected much as he stood to read from the Scriptures and share a few thoughts.

"My dear friends," he said, "this is a simple text indeed. It says, 'Look.' Now lookin' don't take a deal of pains. It ain't liftin' your foot or your finger. It is just 'Look.' Well a man needn't go to college to learn to look. You may be the biggest fool, and yet you can look. Anyone can look: Even a child can look. But then the text says, 'Look unto Me.' Ay! Many on ye are lookin' to yourselves, but it's no use lookin' there. You'll never find comfort in yourselves. Some look to God the Father. No, look to Him by-and-by. Jesus Christ says, 'Look unto Me.' Some of ye say, 'We must wait for the Spirit's workin'.' You have no business with that just now. Look to *Christ*. The text says, 'Look unto *Me*.' "

It took only ten minutes for the man to deliver his message. But as he spoke, he noticed a visitor sitting in a side pew, a boy about fourteen or fifteen years old. The boy's name was Charles. When the storm blew in, Charles had been in route to a more fashionable church in another part of town. But seeing he couldn't make it there, he had ducked inside the little Methodist church instead.

Closing his talk, the man fixed his eyes on Charles and said, "Young man, you look miserable. You will always be miserable if you don't obey my text; but if you obey now, this moment you will be saved." Then the man lifted his hands and shouted with great passion, "Young man, look to Jesus Christ! Look! Look! Look! You have nothing to do but look and live."

This was all Charles needed to hear. That very moment he encountered the incredible freedom and simplicity of the gospel. For several years, he had struggled with his decision for Christ. Suddenly he realized that all the other things he had been doing to find God would never work. To his great relief, Charles learned that all he had to do was *look to Jesus*. Speaking of this experience years later, Charles said, "I thought I could dance all the way home. I could understand what John Bunyan meant when he declared he wanted to tell the crows on the ploughed land all about his conversion. He was too full to hold. He must tell somebody."

And tell somebody is exactly what Charles did. A few weeks later, he preached his first sermon. By the time he was seventeen, the church he pastored was filled to overflowing. At nineteen, he was called to a large, historic church in London. And when he was twenty-six, Charles Spurgeon built the Metropolitan Tabernacle, the largest Baptist church in the world at that time. He often preached ten times a day. He oversaw a pastors' college, several orphanages, and various schools and missions. He produced a magazine and wrote more than eighty books. Tens of thousands gave their lives to Christ, entered full-time ministry, or served in foreign missions as a result of Spurgeon's preaching. The influence of his life and work was felt around the world. He has been ranked in the company of Augustine, John Calvin, and Martin Luther. Even now, 150 years later, Spurgeon is still called "the prince of preachers."

Young Charles Spurgeon was a first-prize catch for the kingdom of God. And all God used to reel him in was a faithful man with a few choice words—and a detour in a snowstorm.

YOU MIGHT LIKE TO KNOW

Speaking of his life before Christ, Spurgeon once said, "I must confess that I never would have been saved if I could have helped it. As long as I ever could, I rebelled, and revolted, and struggled against God. When He would have me pray, I would not pray, and when He would have me listen to the sound of ministry, I would not. And when I heard, and the tear rolled down my cheek, I wiped it away and defied Him to melt my soul. But long before I began with Christ, He began with me."

Spurgeon's mother once said, "What a mercy that boy was converted when he was young."[1]

The Picture Worth More Than a Thousand Souls

Words are potential art,
ready to be performed on the interior stage of our minds.
—FLORENCE LITTAUER

It was in a European art gallery that Nicholas von Zinzendorf first found his life's work. He wasn't a painter, sculptor, or patron of the arts. Neither was he an architect, historian, nor museum curator. In fact, the profession Nicholas discovered in the art gallery had nothing to do with art.

Nicholas happened to be perusing through paintings this particular day because it was the sort of thing German counts were expected to do in the eighteenth century. And, as it was with every other young German nobleman, much was expected of Count Nicholas von Zinzendorf.

Count Zinzendorf had been born into a wealthy, aristocratic family. When his father died, his mother remarried and left him in the care of his aunt and grandmother. These women instilled in Nicholas a love for God and kindled his interest in spiritual things.

When he was ten years old, Nicholas was sent to study at the University of Halle. There he joined a group of dedicated youths to form the Order of the Mustard Seed, a Christian fraternity whose sole purpose was to love the whole human family and to spread the gospel of Christ. After graduating from Halle, Nicholas studied at the University of Wittenburg, where he was groomed for a much-anticipated role in the service of the state. But the life of a German nobleman did not appeal to Nicholas. He much preferred the idea of Christian ministry. However, due to expectations and family tradition, entering the ministry was out of the question.

It was during this time of vocational unhappiness that the count was on a tour of Europe and happened into an art gallery. In the gallery, he came upon a painting by Domenico Feti called *Ecce Homo,* which depicted Christ wearing the crown of thorns. The artwork was exquisite; however, it was not the artist's technique that captured Nicholas's attention. His eyes were drawn to these words inscribed at the bottom of the painting: "All this I did for you, what are you doing for me?"[2]

Immediately Count Zinzendorf knew he had received a message from God, and he knew what he had to do. He was to turn his back on the opinions of men and surrender his life to the King of Kings.

Three years later, amid the protests of his neighbors, Count Zinzendorf opened his personal estate to a group of Protestant refugees. Over time, word of his generosity spread, and other Christian exiles joined them. Before long, these believers formed the beginning of the Moravian movement.

In 1727, a great spiritual awakening visited the Moravian congregation, and as a result, they received a passionate calling to missions. This evangelistic zeal was to set the stage for amazing events that followed.

While attending the coronation of the Danish king Christian VI, two men from Greenland and a Negro slave from the West Indies approached Count Zinzendorf. Their appeal for spiritual assistance so moved him that within the year he sent the first two Moravian missionaries to the Virgin Islands. During the next twenty years, Zinzendorf proceeded to commission more missionaries than all the Protestants and Anglicans had in the previous two hundred years.

In 1740, Count Zinzendorf sailed for the colonies to supervise mission work among the American Indians. By the time he returned to Germany, he had secured twenty more missionaries for the cause.

Count Zinzendorf has been called one of the greatest missionary statesmen of all time. It is estimated that he did more to advance the cause of Protestant missionaries in the eighteenth century than anyone else. In fact, his influence is said to have equaled or surpassed even that of his friends John Wesley and George Whitefield. Zinzendorf was the pioneer of ecumenical evangelism, founder of the Moravian Church, and author of a number of hymns. He has been credited as being the first to spark the flame for worldwide missions and the person most responsible for setting the stage for men like William Carey, the famous missionary to India.

The spiritual legacy of Count Nicholas von Zinzendorf is quite amazing. But what may be even more incredible is the knowledge that twelve thought-provoking words at the bottom of a painting were all God used to bring it to pass.

YOU MIGHT LIKE TO KNOW

The village Count Zinzendorf founded on his estate was called Herrnhut, which means "the Lord's watch." In 1727, a twenty-four-hour prayer vigil began at Herrnhut and continued uninterrupted for more than one hundred years. John Wesley, the founder of the Methodist Church, credits the Moravians he met on board ship to America for his own spiritual awakening.

∞

Minister of Imagination

So deep and meaningful is the joy and enthusiasm
that is born in one's mind and heart by human love
and helpfulness that it has the power to motivate for a lifetime.
—NORMAN VINCENT PEALE

One summer, while other little boys played baseball, splashed in the creek, or chased ice-cream trucks, Fred was stuck in his room. He wasn't in trouble; he had hay fever. And his loving, overprotective mother had thought up a scheme to cure him. Day and night, for an entire summer, Fred was to breathe the air in a specially equipped, air-conditioned room. It was a valiant effort. However, the greatest gain of Fred's three-month solitary confinement came not to his body, but to his highly imaginative brain.

Fred was born in a small industrial town in western Pennsylvania, and until the age of eleven, when his parents adopted a baby girl, he was the only child in the large, red brick house on Weldon Street. His father was the president of a silica brick company in the area, and due to Fred's frequent illnesses, his mother always made sure he was properly dressed and cared for.

Fred's mother was a somewhat fearful woman who never allowed him to play outdoors unsupervised. As a result, he had a fairly lonely childhood, which only served to fuel his budding creativity. To keep himself occupied, Fred spent hours practicing the piano and making up plays with his puppets and lead soldiers.

One of the true joys of Fred's childhood was his grandfather, the man he was named for, Fred McFeely. When Fred was with his grandfather, he felt free to run and play. His grandfather often had some new and fascinating discovery to reveal to him.

One time, as Fred was leaving a particularly delightful visit, his grandfather spoke words that would stick with him his whole life. In fact, the comment so impressed Fred that it became the central theme of his entire professional career.

After high school, Fred left Pennsylvania to study music composition at Rollins College in Winter Park, Florida. It was there that he met his wife, Joanne. During Fred's senior year, he made plans to attend Pittsburgh Theological Seminary, but in 1951, while home for spring break, he saw something that stopped him in his tracks.

It was television.

Though he had no stomach for the pie-throwing programs he saw on the set, the medium itself fascinated Fred. He had an idea there might be some redeeming value in it, a platform to share a worthier message. So upon graduation, instead of heading for seminary, he traveled to New York City to learn the business of television.

For two years, he worked with such shows as the *NBC Opera Theatre*, *The Hit Parade*, and *The Kate Smith Hour*. Fred enjoyed significant advancement until he surprised everyone by leaving NBC for a very risky venture. The nation's first publicly owned television station, WQED-TV in Pittsburgh, was going on the air, and Fred wanted to be part of it. When people questioned the wisdom of this radical move, Fred replied, "Something tells me this is what I'm supposed to do."

In Pittsburgh, Fred helped write and produce *The Children's Corner* program, and in his off-hours, he studied theology and child psychology. It was this unique blend of technology, theology, and psychology that formed the basis for a new fifteen-minute program called *Misterogers*, which was produced by Canadian Broadcasting in 1963.

Today *Mister Rogers' Neighborhood* is broadcast on more than three hundred stations, is watched in more than eight million households, and has been running for thirty-three consecutive years.

Some time ago, the students at a Boston College commencement exercise cheered Fred wildly as he stood to give the invocation. The ovation lasted several minutes, then it broke into a wave. Finally Fred leaned into the microphone and, in his naturally gentle voice, asked, "Will you sing with me?" The students, who had all learned the song as little children, locked arms together and obediently sang, "It's a beautiful day in this neighborhood," along with him.

By now Fred was getting familiar with this kind of response. He had already received twenty-five honorary doctorate degrees.

Mr. Rogers is in his seventies now, and he still produces approximately three weeks of new programming a year. He personally answers each letter he receives and uses the same puppets and sets he began with more than three decades ago. In a world of razzle-dazzle, high-tech kid shows, Fred still believes that the most effective means of building a child's self-esteem is a deliberate, repetitive, one-on-one approach. Scholars agree. Two Yale psychologists comparing

Sesame Street and *Mister Rogers' Neighborhood* concluded that children follow the *Neighborhood* stories better than the slicker, faster-paced *Sesame Street* ones. They also found that the play of kids watching *Mister Rogers' Neighborhood* was much more imaginative.

And imagination is Fred Rogers's specialty.

Want to know the life-defining comment spoken by his wise and loving grandfather as Fred Rogers left him that day so long ago? If you've ever watched *Mister Rogers' Neighborhood,* you already know the answer. They were the same words he has used to close every one of his programs for more than thirty years: "You know, you've made this day a special day by just your being you. There's only one person in the whole world like you. And people can like you exactly as you are."[3]

YOU MIGHT LIKE TO KNOW

One of the regular characters in *Mister Rogers' Neighborhood* is named Mr. McFeely, after Fred Rogers's grandfather. Fred is an ordained Presbyterian minster who fully believes that the children and parents who watch his program are his God-given congregation. His mother made most of the signature cardigan sweaters he wears on his program. Fred has won three Emmy awards and, in 1998, was awarded the highest honor in television, the Lifetime Achievement Award. Standing to receive the award, Mr. Rogers looked at the audience and said, "All of us have special ones who have loved us into being. Would you take, along with me, ten seconds to think of the people who have helped you become who you are...ten seconds of silence. I'll watch the time." Exactly ten seconds later, he concluded by saying, "May God be with you," then he left the stage.[4]

A Call in the Wild

Here is a good searching question for a man to ask himself as he reviews his
past life: Have I written in the snow?
Will my life work endure the lapse of years and the fret of change?
Has there been anything immortal in it,
which will survive the speedy wreck of all sublunary things?

—CHARLES SPURGEON

Every summer, kids all over the world head for camp—a seemingly harmless endeavor. At camp, they paddle canoes and spray shaving cream, and if it's a Christian camp, they learn a few things about God. The parents of these kids are usually happy with this arrangement, thinking, with some nostalgia, that a week or two at camp is bound to be good for their child. Bill's parents probably thought this. Little did they know that one of their son's trips to camp would dash their hopes for his future and influence millions of lives.

Bill grew up in Michigan, the son of a highly successful produce-company owner. It was a commonly understood fact that one day Bill would inherit the helm of the family business, so his father seized every opportunity to nurture the skills and mind-set of a world-class entrepreneur.

By the time Bill was in kindergarten, he was already accompanying his father to work on Saturdays, where he sorted vegetables and washed refrigerator bins. In the first grade, while most of his friends played with toy pickup trucks, Bill learned to drive the real thing. Then, to teach him confidence and survival skills, Bill's dad sent him off to Colorado for a ski vacation without alerting him that his train would stop twenty-five miles from his destination. Bill made the trip alone at the ripe old age of ten. By seventh grade, he and a friend were sailing the family boat across Lake Michigan.

As Bill grew older, he was stretched and worked even more. During high school, he would leave Michigan on Friday night, drive a semi to Florida for a produce pickup, and return home Monday morning just in time to make his first class. When school let out, he managed migrant crews on the family farms.

But there was adventure too. As a sixteen-year-old, Bill flew solo in the family plane. And once not long after that he was handed a ticket for an eight-week tour of Europe and Africa.

However, during this season of his life, travel and toys were not the only focus of Bill's life. On a predestined parallel track, God was plowing inroads to his soul.

Each summer, Bill attended a church camp in Wisconsin, and it was there, at the age of seventeen, that he finally grasped the radical nature of God's love and made a personal commitment to Jesus Christ. Describing this experience years later, Bill said, "I thought my heart was going to explode. I couldn't imagine that kind of love. I remember just standing there saying, 'You've got to be kidding. This is too good to be true. If this is real, this is the greatest thing on the face of the earth.'"

For a while, Bill's passion for the good life and his commitment to Christ peacefully coexisted. But little by little, the fabric of the future he'd planned began to fray. Then a question was put to him that led to the hardest decision of his life.

While Bill was in college, he went again to summer camp—this time as a counselor, lifeguard, and Bible study leader. One day a man named Art, the director of a Christian youth association, cornered Bill and asked, "What are you doing with your life?"

"I do a little work. I do a little play. I have a little sweetheart. I raise a little Cain on Fridays and Saturdays. Then I go to church on Sundays," was Bill's response.

"Get serious, Bill. What are you doing with your life that matters? What are you doing that will last forever?"

At the time, Bill didn't have a good answer. But the question continued to nag him. Then, one night, a short time later, as he was in South America visiting missionary friends of his father, Bill sat in a restaurant overlooking Copacabana Beach in Rio de Janeiro. During his meal he overheard the conversation of an older couple sitting near him. They were celebrating the fact that all their years of hard work had finally culminated in an exotic trip and dinner in a fine restaurant. The scene seemed sad to Bill. A lifetime of work for a trip and some food? That night, he went back to his room, got on his knees, and prayed, "God, there's got to be more to my life than this."[5]

Nearly thirty-five years later, it's an understatement to say that Bill Hybels "got a life." Today he is the founding and senior pastor of Willow Creek Community Church in Barrington, Illinois, the largest church in North America. Approximately seventeen thousand people attend the weekend services. He is most noted for spearheading what has become known as the worldwide "seeker" movement. Now more than fifty-five hundred churches in the Willow Creek Association embrace Bill's vision of relevant New Testament Christianity and passionately identify with the Christ-patterned phrase that he often champions: "People matter to God."

Most kids go to camp and come home with a few new friends

and some photographs. But sometimes, something God-powered happens there. Sometimes a gauntlet is thrown, the challenge is accepted, and a fresh, new face in church history appears.

YOU MIGHT LIKE TO KNOW

Bill Hybels's start in ministry came as a youth pastor at South Park Church in Park Ridge, Illinois. Within three years, South Park Church was reaching twelve hundred high-school students. After its first year, Willow Creek Community Church saw one thousand in attendance. This year, they celebrate twenty-five years of "seeker-driven" ministry. Bill is the author of numerous books, including *Rediscovering Church* and *Fit to Be Tied* with his wife, Lynne, *Becoming a Contagious Christian* with Mark Mittleburg, and *The Heart of a Leader* and *Leadership by the Book* with Ken Blanchard. Bill served for five years as chaplain of the Chicago Bears. He and Lynne have two college-age children who also serve in vital Willow Creek ministries.

∞

An Unsuspecting Prophet Hits It on the Numbers

Spoken words of blessing should start in the delivery room and continue throughout life.

—JOHN TRENT AND GARY SMALLEY

When a baby is born, people like to predict a certain destiny for the child. They say, "Look at those fingers. I bet she'll be a pianist one day." Or, "Look at his wild hair! I bet he's another Einstein." Ninety-nine percent of the time, these remarks are casual and lighthearted, and in a few years, everyone forgets what was said. But there was a time when the prediction of one unsuspecting prophet came incredibly true.

It was September 1954, and the maternity ward at St. John's Hospital in Tulsa, Oklahoma, was booming with "Sooner" babies. As usual, there were a smattering of preemies in the back and a row of average-sized newborns lined up at the viewing window. But the biggest little guy in the bunch weighed in at a bouncing ten pounds, four ounces. This baby, whose parents had named him Steve, made such an impression on the staff that one of the nurses bought the little infant a tiny toy football. As she placed the ball in baby Steve's bassinet, she proclaimed, "This boy is going to be a player!"[6]

Now this kind of statement is not an uncommon occurrence. It's no secret that Oklahomans are fanatical about football. What makes this prophecy so significant is how superbly it was fulfilled.

However, before the would-be football player could reach this lofty goal, he would face his share of obstacles.

In grade school, Steve was only average in size—not exactly an advantage for someone slated to be a football player. Then his parents divorced, and his mother remarried an alcoholic who frequently moved the family and fought physically with his mother in front the children. At one point the violence got so bad that Steve's mother asked him, "What should I do?" He thought to himself, *I don't know. I'm only in the tenth grade.*

As a high-school sophomore, Steve was one of 150 guys who tried out for the Putnam City High School football team. He wasn't considered big enough or fast enough to play the coveted halfback position, so Steve decided to quit. But when his mom discovered his intention, she sat him down at the breakfast table and encouraged him to stick it out. Her talk changed his mind. Steve decided to go out for a different position, one more suited to his abilities. It was the best decision he could have made, one that would eventually make him a household name.

That year Steve Largent became a wide receiver, and it was in that position that his grit and willingness to dive for the tough catches began to win him recognition.

Steve was far from a high-school football standout, but when he graduated, a few colleges were willing to offer him a scholarship. He chose the University of Tulsa, and the school was richly rewarded for its investment when Steve led the nation in touchdown receptions his junior and senior years.

Even with this outstanding achievement, the professional scouts were not impressed with Steve's limited size and lack of quickness. It wasn't until the fourth round of the NFL draft that he was chosen by the Houston Oilers. However, the next summer, Steve was cut from their roster.

By this time, Steve's former coach from the University of Tulsa had moved on to a spot on the staff of the Seattle Seahawks. At his urging, the Pacific Coast team was willing to take a look at Steve. After a shaky tryout, Steve won a spot on the team and continued to play for the Seahawks his entire illustrious career.

The big baby in the St. John's Hospital bassinet only turned out to be five-foot-eleven and 190 pounds—not much if you look at today's player statistics. But Steve's sturdy frame carried him through fourteen hard-hitting years in professional football. He held six major NFL career pass-receiving records, and when he retired in 1989, Steve was the all-time NFL receptions leader. He caught a pass in 177 consecutive games, and in 1995, Steve was the first Seattle Seahawk to be inducted into the NFL Hall of Fame.

Today Steve Largent dodges defenders on an even more challenging field: politics. At his wife's insistence, Steve ran for the United States Congress in 1994 and won by a decided margin. He is currently serving his third term, representing the First Congressional District of Oklahoma as a conservative Republican and a devoted Christian husband and father.

Maybe the words and gift from a kindhearted nurse had no bearing at all on Steve Largent's calling in life. But then again, maybe they did.

YOU MIGHT LIKE TO KNOW

Steve Largent never made it to the Super Bowl, but in 1988, he became a champion of the all-American cereal bowl when he was featured on the front of a Wheaties box. Steve met both his sweetheart, Terry, and his Savior, Jesus Christ, at a high-school Young Life meeting. He is the proud father of four children. In 1982, Steve angered some of his teammates by announcing he would not honor a players' strike if one were called. "I'm a Christian," he explained to the media, "and God's Word calls a contract a vow."[7]

A CALLING FROM GOD'S WORD

When Jesus reached the spot, he looked up and said to him,
"Zacchaeus, come down immediately. I must stay at your house today."
—LUKE 19:5

It builds courage to know that when Jesus calls us out of the crowd to join him in his work, he accepts us right where we are. He knows that we question our own competency. He is aware of our insecurities. And the first thing he does to alleviate our fear is to call us by name. Jesus, better than anyone, knows the value of personal acknowledgment.

Just as it was with Zacchaeus, in spite of our limitations and liabilities, before we've even proven ourselves, Christ writes our name on his roster and adds us to his team. But he makes one request before we take the field. He asks us to sit down and have a meal with him so we can power up, talk over strategy, and calm our shaky nerves.

No matter where we have been or where he found us, if Christ has singled us out, sooner or later he will hand us a mandate to motivate others. He will call us to light up the darkness, to shine like stars in the universe, and to hold out his marvelous life.

BOOST YOUR OWN WORD POWER

Cultivate relationships with young people. Step out and challenge them to be the best they can be for God. Look into their lives and comment on the goodness that you see there. Take some time to affirm their unique and God-planned place in history. Cultivate faithfulness. Revel in the rhythm of ordinary things. Scripture shows us that Christ's favorite earth-side hangouts were the common places—the kinds of places where we feel the most natural and relaxed, the places we are freest to express our hearts. Embrace the days of bite-size beginnings, tedious tasks, and mandatory meetings. At these non-eventful times in our lives, the words we speak are often our most thoughtful, passionate, and real. It is likely that when we expect it least, God can use us most.

My son, pay attention to my wisdom,
listen well to my words of insight.

—PROVERBS 5:1

3

CHOICE WORDS OF COUNSEL

A Father's Fundamentals

When I think of those who have influenced my life the most,
I think not of the great but of the good.

—JOHN KNOX

There is a buzz in the air. It is graduation day at Johnny's little three-room grade school, and everyone is getting dressed to go. Johnny has on his best denim overalls in honor of the event. But before the family heads out, his dad has a gift for him.

Out of his pocket comes a crumpled two-dollar bill that his dad has been saving. Handing it to his wide-eyed son, he says, "Johnny, as long as you have this, you'll never be broke."

Johnny smiles, thanks his father, and holds on to that two-dollar bill for a long time, long enough for him to grow up, get married, and pass it to his own boy one day.

But that's not all. There is something else Johnny's dad wants to give him. It isn't a bike or a gun or a new hat. It is a card. On this card, he has written his guidelines for life. He lives by these rules and wants to make sure that Johnny knows the most valuable thing he can ever acquire is virtue.

There is no speech. His dad just gives him the card and says, "Son, try to live up to these things."

On one side is a poem by Henry Van Dyke. It's a short rhyme that reminds Johnny to think clearly, love sincerely, act purely, and trust God securely. Then on the flip side is his father's personal creed. The top of the card reads: "Seven Things to Do." Johnny knows the seven things; he has seen them in action every single day of his life. But now he has them in writing. Something about seeing it on the card makes a lasting impression on the boy. The list reads:

1. Be true to yourself.
2. Help others.
3. Make each day your masterpiece.
4. Drink deeply from good books, especially the Bible.
5. Make friendship a fine art.
6. Build a shelter against a rainy day.
7. Pray for guidance and count and give thanks for your blessings every day.

Johnny folded the card and stuck it in his pocket that day, along with the two-dollar bill. And seventy years later, he is still carrying it.

As best he could, Johnny lived by his father's guidelines. And when he became a teacher, father, and coach, he was almost as famous for his character as he was for his remarkable achievements.

Growing up, Johnny lived on a farm with no electricity or indoor plumbing. But they did have two mules named Jack and

Kate. Sometimes Kate would get stubborn and lie down when she was supposed to be plowing. This would always frustrate Johnny. He would yank and yell but get no results. Then his father would start walking across the field. He would get close enough for the animal to hear him say, "Kate." That was all. At that word, the mule would get up and go back to work. Johnny learned a life lesson from this: A soft tongue is often more effective than a sharp one.

Everyone on the farm worked hard. They raised corn, hay, wheat, tomatoes, and watermelons. But at night, after working all day in the fields, after dinner was done, Johnny's dad read poetry to the family.

There were fun times too. Their farm was in Indiana, the epicenter for basketball in America. And when the boys finished their chores, they played a crude form of basketball in the barn. Johnny's dad had tacked an old tomato basket to the hayloft, which made a good rim with the bottom punched out. His mom made the ball from rags stuffed in black cotton hose.

As time went by, Johnny got pretty good at playing ragtag basketball. He made the squad in high school, where his coach, Glenn Curtis, drilled the fundamentals. In college, Johnny played for Purdue University, where he was named an All-American three years in a row and awarded College Player of the Year.

Johnny's accomplishments got a good deal of publicity. One day, in his senior year, the Celtics offered him a job playing in professional basketball for five thousand dollars a year. Five thousand dollars a year was more money than he could imagine. A teaching job with some coaching on the side would only bring in fifteen hundred dollars. So the Celtics' offer was tempting.

Piggy Lambert was Johnny's coach at the time. He was a wise and principled man, so hoping for some advice, Johnny dropped by to see him.

After hearing about the Celtics' offer, the coach shuffled a few papers on his desk then said, "That's a lot of money, isn't it, John?"

Johnny laughed. "Yes, it sure is, Coach. It's a lot of money."

The coach paused for a minute then said, "Is that what you came to Purdue for?"

"What do you mean, Coach?"

"I mean, did you come to this university so you could travel around in professional athletics?"

"No, I didn't come here to do that, sir. I came to get an education."

"Well, then maybe you should use it," the coach said. "But that's a decision you'll have to make for yourself."[1]

Johnny chose not to play professional basketball. And in years to come, thousands of players, students, and college basketball fans would be glad he didn't. Instead of going pro, Johnny taught high-school English and coached basketball. Later, he taught and coached at Indiana State Teachers College.

Then one day, by a strange mistake, he took the job that would write his name in the record books.

At the time, two colleges wanted Johnny to coach for them: One was the University of Minnesota, and the other was UCLA. Johnny wanted to go to Minnesota, and he was ready to accept the job if the details could be worked out. So a date was set for a phone call to confirm the decision. But just in case that job fell through, Johnny had also scheduled a backup call from UCLA. Minnesota was due to call at 6:00 P.M., and UCLA was set for 7:00. At 6:00, the phone didn't ring. Then came 6:15 and 6:45 and still no call from Minnesota. Johnny didn't know it at the time, but a snow-storm in Minnesota had shut down all the phone lines. At 7:00 on the nose, UCLA called. Since Johnny hadn't heard from Minnesota, he assumed the deal was off. UCLA won the toss. And—by an act of God—the legendary John Wooden became their new head basketball coach. Though he would rather have gone to Minnesota, John headed to UCLA because he had already given them his word.

For the first fifteen seasons that John Wooden coached the Bruins, he couldn't win a national championship. Then suddenly the tide changed, and no one could stop him from winning them. His first national championship came in 1964. Then from 1967 to 1973, he took seven straight national championships. By the end of his career, John's teams had won an unprecedented ten national championships, making him the winningest college basketball coach in history.[2]

But equal to or surpassing all his impressive wins was the effect Wooden had on his family, players, and staff. As a leader, he was known for his work ethic, enthusiasm, and attention to detail. He brought out the best in everyone. And just as his father would have liked, he is perhaps most remembered by them as a kind, soft-spoken man of rare and exceptional character.

YOU MIGHT LIKE TO KNOW

John Wooden coached at UCLA for twenty-seven years. His career win-loss record was 885–203. He is the only person to be entered into the Basketball Hall of Fame twice.

John Smith, a UCLA track coach, was known for slipping in to watch John Wooden conduct his basketball practices. Of them he said, "[John] had the patience of Job. If you didn't get his message, he just repeated it. He reprimanded so softly you reflected on your own character." Of Wooden, Dennis Crum, former Wooden assistant and head basketball coach at the University of Louisville, said, "His life away from basketball has been dominated by his family and church.... I guess it would suffice to say that along with my father, he has had a tremendous influence on my life. To try to emulate him both on and off the floor is very difficult to do. I...can only pray that I can have half as much influence on the young people I coach as he has had on me."[3]

NBA Hall of Famer and former UCLA basketball player Bill Walton said, "I was touched by Coach Wooden's greatness—he set a standard I have been trying to live up to ever since. He is as positive as you get. He taught values and characteristics that could make us not only good players but good people.... I'm telling my four teenage sons what [he] used to tell his players. I'm even writing his maxims on their lunch bags."[4]

∞

More Power to Him

Few things in the world are more powerful than a positive push. A smile. A word of optimism and hope. A "you can do it" when things are tough.
—RICH DEVOS

A little boy scampers across the front porch when he sees a car drive up in the yard. His uncle jumps out and bounds up the steps to meet him. It's the first time they've laid eyes on each other because the uncle has been in China since before the child was born. The uncle is tall and good looking and full of life. He runs up to the little boy, tussles his hair, then takes him firmly by the shoulders and says, "Well, I guess you're Bob! I think you are going to be a preacher someday." Bob is only four years old, but that night he adds a new wish to his prayer list: "And dear God, make me a preacher when I grow up!"

With his words, Bob's uncle has started something big. But it will be years before anyone knows just how big.

Amazingly, Bob did make the ministry his vocation. After a few years of pastoring near Chicago, he and his wife traveled to Orange County, California, to consider starting a new church there. Everything in California was booming, but the decision to uproot and start all over was a risky one. As Bob prayed about what to do, the words of a great church leader he had studied in seminary, George Truett, suddenly came back to him. Truett said, "The greatest churches have yet to be organized."

Those words were all the challenge Bob needed. The decision to move was made.

But startup church life in California was anything but easy. Land prices were enormous, and all the school auditoriums in the area were already taken on Sunday. It looked like Bob would have to get creative if he were going to grow a church here. Then he remembered attending a service at a drive-in movie theater in Iowa. It gave him an idea. Bob began to make plans to hold his services at the Orange Drive-in Theater.

Most of Bob's preacher friends were skeptical. "People won't come to a drive-in church," they warned him. But Bob packed up an organ and a seventy-dollar sound system and carted it all to the drive-in anyway. Then the day came. After much hopeful prayer, about fifty cars showed up as Bob stood on the roof of the snack bar and delivered his now-famous message, "If you have faith as a grain of mustard seed, you can say to this mountain move, and nothing will be impossible unto you."[5]

Eighteen months later, Bob and his fledgling congregation built a new chapel, and he began preaching in both locations on Sundays. After four years, he was ready to merge the two services. But his new church would have the old elements. Why not purposely make provision for people who want to stay in their cars at the new location? He had heard of a church in Florida putting loudspeakers in the parking lot when they outgrew their facilities. It was a radical move, but he wanted to give it a try.

Bob began to imagine a new auditorium with a huge glass wall, gardens, fountains, acres of trees, and a large enough parking lot for attendees to stay in their cars if they wished. Soon ten acres of property was located for sixty-six thousand dollars. In order to purchase the land, the church would have to come up with nineteen thousand dollars in only four months. Bob believed God was in it. And amidst opposition, they prayed their way to the eleventh hour, just before the down payment was due. After all the gifts and pledges were in, they were still short three thousand dollars. It looked like the project would have to be scrubbed. Then a suggestion came from Bob's wife: Why not call one of their very first church members? Bob was dubious, but her counsel came from God. The call was made, the money was secured, and the plans went forth for a million-dollar building to the glory of God.

The building took two years to complete. On November 5, 1961, Dr. Norman Vincent Peale flew in from New York to preach the first sermon in the new, innovative facilities of the Garden Grove Community Church.

Eight years later, in 1969, Bob was assisting with one of the Billy Graham crusades and received a piece of advice that would launch his ministry into the next galaxy. Bob had known Billy for a long time. The two of them were walking together when they passed one of the television trucks used for broadcasting the crusade.

"C'mon," Billy said, "let me show you how we tape these things. You ought to televise your church service."[6] As they viewed the truck, Billy Graham challenged Dr. Robert Schuller to raise two hundred thousand dollars from his congregation on a single Sunday and start a TV ministry. Robert was at first reluctant, but when he finally asked the church to give, the people pledged even more than what was needed. Robert took it as a sign. And a brand-new day dawned in Christian television.

This year, the *Hour of Power* television ministry will mark its thirtieth year of broadcasting. It is the fourth-longest-running program in television history and is watched by an astounding thirty million viewers worldwide.[7]

YOU MIGHT LIKE TO KNOW

Dr. Robert Schuller is the author of thirty-two books, five of which have appeared on the *New York Times* bestseller list. Among the numerous awards he has received are the Horatio Alger Award, Clergyman of the Year, Award of Excellence for Religious Media, and the Peacemaker Award. He is on the board of the Guild of Architects of the American Institute of Architects, Board of Counselors for the YMCA, and the Advisory Board of Church Growth International in Seoul, South Korea. He has honorary doctorates from at least six colleges and universities. He and his wife, Arvella, have five children and seventeen grandchildren.

Their son Robert Anthony has been announced as Dr. Schuller's future successor.[8]

∞

Shaped by the Words of a Slave

There lies in each of us a hero awaiting the call to action.
—H. JACKSON BROWN JR.

Mariah Watkins had delivered more babies than any other woman in town. But for all she knew about babies, she had borne no child of her own. Perhaps that's why she was willing to take in the stray boy who showed up one day at her barn.

The boy she took in was a genius, but she couldn't tell it by looking at him. True, he seemed different from other children, more frail and sensitive. But Mariah didn't see what the entire world would someday come to know about George. She just saw a child in need of a home and was willing to give it to him.

George had come to her town to go to school. When they wouldn't allow him in the white school where he lived, he traveled eight miles to attend an all-black school located just across the street from the home of Mariah and her husband, Andrew.

The next day, George told Mariah that he was lucky to have picked her barn to sleep in that night. But the woman said, "Luck had nothing to do with it, boy. God brought you to my yard. He has work for you, and he wants Andrew and me to lend a hand."[9]

At lunchtime, George would hop over the fence to help Mariah with the laundry. Besides giving him room and board, she taught

George about herbs, roots, and other natural medicines. She honed his cooking and cleaning skills and even taught him to knit and crochet. One Christmas, she gave him an old, tattered Bible and made sure he read it every day. Unlike most former slave women, Mariah could read—thanks to a slave named Libby who had taught her by lamplight in spite of the beating she could get for doing it. Libby was one of Mariah's heroes, and the times George stayed home from school sick, Mariah would tell him about Libby's selfless dedication to her people.

It was during one of these storytelling sessions that Mariah spoke to George about his place in the world. Her words lodged deep in his soul and supplied the fuel for the innumerable contributions he would eventually make.

"You must learn all you can," she said, "then be like Libby. Go out in the world and give your learning back to our people. They're starving for a little learning."

George did get all the learning he could. He sucked up every drop of knowledge in the little black school in Neosho, Missouri, then he moved on throughout the Midwest in search of other schools that would take him. For many years, he made money any way he could and then entered Simpson College to study art. While George was there, a teacher noticed something special about him and encouraged him to transfer to Iowa State to study agriculture.

This proved to be another divine intervention.

At Iowa State, George took graduate courses under great professors who recognized his keen mind and mentored him in the fields of botany and mycology. Then as he was nearing completion of his master's degree, a letter came from the famous black educator

Booker T. Washington, a man who was known throughout the country for promising to help Southern blacks rise from poverty. Washington offered George the position of director of the agricultural school and state agricultural experiment station at his famous Tuskegee Institute. He accepted the job, which was the turning point of George's life.

In a letter of response to Washington, George reaffirmed the calling spoken over his life by Mariah Watkins. He said, "It has always been one of the great ideals of my life to be of the greatest good to the greatest number of 'my people' possible and to this end I have been preparing myself for these many years; feeling as I do that this line of education is the key to unlock the golden door of freedom to our people."

When George arrived at Tuskegee, the agricultural department consisted of a butter churn, several starving hogs, acres of worthless soil, and one old horse. So he and his students literally built their school from the ground up, using carved milk cartons, empty cans, and whatever else could be found to construct a working laboratory.

For the next fifty years, George Washington Carver gave his learning back to hundreds and hundreds of "his people" and then, ultimately, to the world. He became as comfortable helping a local farmer as he was advising Ghandi on health issues for India. When the tsetse fly threatened the lives of their cows, George taught African missionaries how to feed people with peanut milk.

His research on the peanut and other vegetables came from his prayer times, and he was famous for marrying the mysticism of religion with the logic of science. He is credited with more than three hundred products from the peanut including milk, cheese, butter, vinegar, coffee, salads, soups, printer's ink, creosote, shampoo, and wood stains. From the sweet potato, he created 118 possibilities, including rubber. From the hard southern clay, he developed paints and pioneered a new science called chemurgy—the industrialization of agricultural products, like wallboard from pine cones, banana stems, and peanut shells. He also created more than fifty dyes from twenty-eight kinds of plants.

By the end of his life, the once-orphaned houseguest of Mariah Watkins had been showered with international acclaim as a botanist, chemurgist, researcher, painter, and inventor. He was a friend of Henry Ford and acquainted with three presidents. Throughout his life, Carver kept a strong faith by constant prayer and daily reading of the same tattered Bible that Mariah had given him as a boy. As a teacher, he sparked a bright hope in his people. And in a time of great unrest, he modeled for his race how to rise above injustice without succumbing to hatred.

YOU MIGHT LIKE TO KNOW

George Washington Carver lived in two rooms of a dormitory at Tuskegee, where books were stacked from floor to the ceiling. He rose at 4:00 A.M. to walk in the woods. By 9:00 A.M., he was in his laboratory and often prayed as he entered, "Open thou mine eyes that I may behold wondrous things out of the law." He experimented with wheat, okra, and artichokes, saying he was interested in them because "God told me to look there."[10] He never accepted a raise and left his life savings of $32,300 to the George Washington Carver Foundation. Carver was an excellent artist. His paintings were exhibited at the Chicago World's Fair and now hang in the George Washington Carver Museum at the Tuskegee Institute in Alabama.

∽

"Do Good in the World and Be Useful"

Let's tell our young people that the best books are yet to be written;
the best paintings have not yet been painted; the best governments are
yet to be formed; the best is yet to be done by them.

—JOHN ERSKINE

Noah was finally going to college. And like most kids headed to an Ivy-League school, his parents had spent the farm, literally, to get him there. Noah's folks had nothing of much value except the family farm, so they mortgaged it to pay for their son's education at Yale.

The day Noah left for college, his mom and dad stopped him at the door. There were proud smiles and brisk hugs, but what Noah remembered most were his parents parting words: "We wish to have you serve your generation and do good in the world and be useful and may [you] so behave as to gain the esteem of all virtuous people…but especially that you may so live as to obtain the favor of the Almighty God and his saving grace in this world and a saving interest in the merits of Jesus Christ, without which no man can be happy."[11]

After a brief interruption to attend the Revolutionary War, Noah finished his studies at Yale. He had planned to attend law school, but this was financially impossible. So he taught school during the day and studied for the bar at night.

The teaching profession was a challenge. Sometimes as many as seventy children were crammed into one classroom. Often there were no desks, and what few textbooks they had were old, outdated ones from England. Noah's solution to the textbook problem was to write his own.

Until this time, there had been no true standardization of English spelling. It was common practice for people to write words the way they sounded, which got complicated since people from different areas spoke with different accents. This was motivation for Noah to begin his work with words. But to him, there was an even more important reason to unify the language. America was a new country, very different in ideas and customs from England. Noah was a dedicated patriot who strongly believed that Americans should form their own new vocabulary, and he set out to make it happen.

First, he wrote a textbook that became known as the *Blue Backed Speller,* and after one hundred years in print, Noah's textbook had sold more than seventy million copies.[12]

Not long after this, one of Noah's old college professors and a trustee of Yale, Rev. Dr. Goodrich, made a life-defining suggestion to Noah. He had seen the reception the country had given Noah's *Blue Backed Speller,* so he put to Noah the thought of attempting a great reference work for the new country. He thought America needed a dictionary that would unify the English language and spelling in a uniquely American way. Americans had come to form their own set of customs and ideas, and he felt that fact should be universally recognized in their language.

Noah agreed. And for more than twenty years, he gave himself to a project that would serve his generation and do volumes of good for the world.

Finally, in 1828, Noah Webster delivered to America the most formidable work of its kind: *An American Dictionary of the English Language.*

The scope of this book required that he live nearly a year in France and England to research word meanings. In England, he discovered that the English dictionaries were at least half a century behind in the subject of science and purposed to bring Americans up to speed with his work. He learned twenty-six languages in order to understand the origins of words. Out of the seventy thousand words he listed in his dictionary, twelve thousand of them were new "American" words never before seen in a dictionary. And from this huge body of knowledge, Americans could now enjoy a standard pronunciation of their version of the English language.

After nearly a lifetime of study, Noah Webster became the unequaled master of words. No other secular book has ever spread so wide and lasted so long. He was called "schoolmaster to America," but in the preface of his monumental accomplishment, he gave glory to God. He wrote: "To that great and benevolent Being, who, during the preparation of this work, has sustained a feeble constitution amidst obstacles and toils, disappointments, infirmities and depression; who has borne me and my manuscripts in safety across the Atlantic, and given me strength…and if the talent which He entrusted to my care, has not been put to the most profitable use in His service, I hope…any misapplication of it may be graciously forgiven."[13]

YOU MIGHT LIKE TO KNOW

After the Bible, Webster's *An American Dictionary of the English Language* has sold more than any other book in American history. In 1833, at the age of seventy-five, Noah published his common version of the Bible, which he translated from the original Hebrew and Greek manuscripts. In the preface of his Bible, Noah stated, "The Bible is the chief moral cause of all that is good, and the best corrector of all that is evil in human society; the best book for regulating the temporal concerns of men, and the only book that can serve as an infallible guide to future felicity."[14]

Noah Webster was the editor of several magazines and wrote scholarly studies on epidemic diseases, mythology, meteors, and European and Asian relations. He was on the first board of trustees for Amherst College. He also wrote *Webster's Biographical Dictionary* and *Webster's Dictionary of Synonyms*. He was a familiar friend of George Washington and James Madison.[15]

A Thousand Tongues of Praise

*The radiating influence from one person
rightly related to God is incalculable.*

—OSWALD CHAMBERS

Charles and his brother were radical men with questionable doctrine, or so their church thought. Though they were both ordained Anglican priests, church leaders believed it best to protect their parishioners from the brothers' teachings on evangelism and salvation by grace. So the men were banned from preaching in nearly every church in England.

This was discouraging at first. Their father had been a priest, and Charles and John had hoped to help the world by following in his footsteps. But in time, the two came to see that their expulsion from the traditional pulpit was a blessing in disguise. It gave them more time to ride horses (an estimated 250,000 miles) and to enjoy the great outdoors. The ban brought them new friends (thousands of them), and what could have looked like the end of their ministry eventually became the most significant spiritual awakening in British history.

It all began at Oxford, where Charles and John Wesley started a club that met for personal spiritual development and religious exercises. In this society, they held each other accountable for their actions and followed strict rules of discipline and piety. They also took mission trips. On one such trip to America, they encountered a Christian sect called the Moravians, who greatly impacted their lives.

Though Charles and John were zealous churchmen, neither had personally accepted Christ as his Savior. The Moravians led the men to salvation and into a deeper relationship with the Holy Spirit. From them, the men became more expressive in their faith and more vibrant in their worship, which disturbed the traditional church.

Forced to take their message outdoors, the two brothers often held meetings in barns, on hillsides, and in fields. Their unconventional outdoor "church" gained an exciting reputation and made it easy for the spiritually curious to investigate Christianity. Before long, thousands would be waiting by the time John or Charles arrived on horseback to preach.

But Charles did more than preach. He had a second talent, one that suddenly began to flourish after he gave his life to Christ. It set him apart from his older brother and made him known as one of the greatest British influences in church history.

Charles wrote hymns.

Hymn writing was a passion for him. He wrote a hymn almost every day of his adult life. By the end of his lifetime, he had written more than sixty-five hundred of them.[16]

One day when he and Peter Bohler, an influential Moravian

leader, were discussing the subject of worship, Charles asked Peter whether he thought it was proper for people to praise God. Peter responded by saying, "Had I a thousand tongues, I would praise him with all."[17]

It was a seemingly innocent comment, but the phrase was a catalyst for exactly what Charles needed to write his most famous hymn. Charles was nearing the eleventh anniversary of his conversion, and he wanted to write a song that would commemorate the day his life was changed forever. So in 1739, Charles Wesley took out his pen and scratched the first words to a new song: "O for a thousand tongues to sing, my great Redeemer's praise, the glories of my God and King, the triumph of his grace!" He didn't stop writing until he had written nineteen verses.

Years later, as John Wesley collected the songs he wanted to include in the first Methodist hymnal, "O for a Thousand Tongues to Sing" was the song he chose for the very first page—a place of honor it kept for many years.

YOU MIGHT LIKE TO KNOW

For seventeen years, Charles Wesley traveled throughout Britain preaching and writing new songs. It is estimated that he and his brother conducted more than forty thousand public services. In all, Charles spent more than fifty years of his life in the ministry. The Moravians are credited with increasing the dimension of zeal and power in the Wesleys' ministry. Even though Charles and his brother were banned from preaching in most of the Anglican churches, they were opposed to any of their followers leaving the organized church. But after John Wesley's death, the English Methodists formally separated from the Church of England and formed the Wesleyan Methodist Church. Other well-known

hymns by Charles Wesley include "Jesus, Lover of My Soul,"
"Hark! The Herald Angels Sing," and "Christ the Lord Is Risen
Today." It is said that even on his deathbed Charles dictated one
last hymn.[18]

∞

Go for the Best

Keep away from people who belittle your ambitions.
Small people always do that, but the really great make
you feel that you too can become great.

—MARK TWAIN

By the looks of things, there was no way Florence was ever
going to college. This was the Depression, and her family didn't
have two nickels to spare in their three-room house at the back of
her father's store. But Florence had her heart set on college, and
she knew there was only one way that she could get there—a
scholarship.

A college scholarship was being offered to one graduating senior at Florence's high school. Florence thought she had a crack at
it, but there was no guarantee. Her grades needed to stay high, and
then somehow she had to get the cash to take a college-prep course
to increase her chances of winning.

But her mother was against the idea.

Katie was a practical woman who wasn't keen on anything
"iffy." The prep course would cost precious money, and after spend-
ing it, Florence still might not win the scholarship. She didn't want
Florence to be disappointed. "Don't get your hopes up too high;

they might get shot down," was one of her unspoken mottoes. Katie wished her daughter were more practical. Why not put the money on a typing course? Everyone knows that secretarial skills would always be in demand. With typing ability, Florence could go anywhere and get a nice job.

But Florence didn't want a nice job. She wanted to go to college.

Throughout this discussion, her father had been lying low, keeping his thoughts to himself, which was usually the safest tack. But he could see that college meant the world to his only daughter, and he, being an optimist, decided that he was willing to take a risk. So he calmly looked up and said, "Florence, I think you should go for it. I think you should always go for the best because it just might happen."

That settled it. Florence would go for the best! She took the college-prep course, studied hard, and finally reached graduation day. As she walked across the stage to receive her diploma, the announcement was made: Florence was the winner of the one-hundred-dollar college scholarship.

After this experience, Florence hit the ground running. She had learned a great lesson that would serve her well for the rest of her life. Now no matter how far-fetched or impossible something seemed, she was determined to go for the best.

At the University of Massachusetts in Amherst, Florence studied English, drama, and speech. She was a natural public speaker. At the age of three, she had recited the entire second chapter of Luke for a Christmas service. Since it appeared to her mother that Florence had no musical talent, she was given elocution lessons instead. For some, this may have felt like a slight, but God did not waste the experience. It was added to the mix of all the other experiences that Florence would need to prepare for his plan for her life.

Florence graduated college with honors and was named Best Female Speaker in New England Colleges her senior year. After graduation, she spent time organizing a new local theater company, directing musical comedies, and working as a high-school speech and drama teacher.

It was during this same time that Florence met Fred, a young man from a prosperous New York family. He was a handsome catch, and his background and social status were miles apart from Florence's. But again she thought, *Why not go for the best?* Soon Florence and Fred were engaged. As the wedding day approached, all the students from her English, drama, and speech classes were enlisted to help with the preparations. Even the shop class pitched in. The whole event created such a stir that *Life* magazine showed up to cover it and published the story on May 18, 1953.

After the wedding, Florence sometimes appeared as a fashion-show commentator for Macy's and continued her involvement with local theater. She was a confident leader and was quickly elected chairman or president of every club she joined. Florence and Fred led the good life. They had everything they needed and more.

Then they began having children.

First came two girls and then a baby boy. But after six months, something seemed terribly wrong with their son. He began crying nonstop and having ten to twelve convulsions a day. After taking him to specialists, they discovered that their beautiful baby had severe brain damage. Florence and Fred were devastated. Soon the child became too sick for them to manage alone, and they were forced to take him to a home. He died within a year.

But in time, Fred and Florence rejoiced again at the birth of a second son. Then six months later, the roof caved in as doctors reported that this child had the same disease.

Florence had always been a strong, capable woman, but this second blow completely leveled her. She tried to press through, but the pain and sadness wouldn't let up. Months of depression set in. All the money they had, the fine home they owned, the nice cars they drove, and their classy, uniformed maid all seemed trite in comparison to the magnitude of their loss.

One day in an effort to help, Florence's sister-in-law invited her to a Christian Women's Club meeting. When Florence arrived, she studied the well-dressed women and wondered what made them all happy. Then as the keynote speaker gave his message, Florence began to feel her bruised and battered heart being wooed by a loving God. At the end of his talk, the man asked if anyone wanted to invite Jesus Christ to be the Lord and Savior of her life. With tears in her eyes, Florence said yes.

Before long, Fred also gave his life to Christ. Now both of them were poised and ready for God's greater plan to be revealed.

Fred had owned a nightclub called Good Time Charlie's, and some months after he became a Christian, he felt compelled to shut it down. The small church they had joined needed a new place to meet, so Fred reopened the building to hold services there. Later, the couple flew to San Bernadino, California, to attend a Campus Crusade for Christ Lay Institute for Evangelism. While they were there, God led them in a radically new direction. Fred was offered a staff position as the conference services director, and soon their young family was headed west.

In California, Florence taught Sunday school and team-taught marriage classes with Fred. Their classes were so popular that they built a new home large enough for a living room that could accommodate one hundred guests for Bible studies.

The invitations flooded in for Florence to speak, and soon she was traveling to women's conferences and retreats all over California. Now, more than thirty years later, the once poor high-school girl who nearly missed her calling to become a typist is one of the foremost Christian speakers and authors in the world.

Since 1984, Florence Littauer and her husband, Fred, have traveled the globe in full-time ministry. Florence's calendar is perpetually full more than a year in advance. And since founding the Christian Leaders, Authors, and Speakers Services (CLASS) in 1981, she has trained thousands of Christian men and women to follow her father's advice to "go for the best" as authors and communicators for Christ. She has been responsible for launching and mentoring a virtual who's who among the most recognized Christian women authors and speakers in America. Among them are Emilie Barnes, Patsy Clairmont, Lee Ezell, Liz Curtis Higgs, Becky Tirabassi, Kathy Collard Miller, and her daughter, Marita Littauer. Florence has authored more than thirty books, including *Personality Plus*, which has sold more than one million copies, *Silver Boxes*, and *Daily Marriage Builders for Couples*, with her husband, Fred.

YOU MIGHT LIKE TO KNOW

Each year, Florence Littauer speaks to approximately fifty to seventy-five groups worldwide and is a guest on many television and radio shows. Many of her books have sold more than one hundred thousand copies, and more than one million copies of her books are in print. She is one of only twenty-three women to receive two of the highest awards given by the National Speakers Association: Certified Speaking Professional and CPAE Speakers Hall of Fame. She has written at least one book per year for the last twenty-five years. Florence and Fred have three children: Lauren, Marita, and Fred Jr. On the darkest days of her life, Florence said, "A jolt like we had with our sons either sends you away from the church or sends you out searching for God. We found God's plan for our life."[19]

GOD'S WORD OF COUNSEL

But Jehoshaphat also said to the king of Israel,
"First seek the counsel of the LORD."

—1 KINGS 22:5

Every day, call-in shows, psychic hotlines, and Internet chat rooms are flooded with people seeking answers to their most pressing pain or conflict. We run to friends or coworkers for quick-fix solutions; if their advice fails, we move to the next person. We call parents or mentors, hoping they will have the magic key to whatever ails us. It seems we'll run almost anywhere, even to strangers, to get help before we do what should be the first thing on our list: Ask God.

God, who is all-knowing, all-loving, and all ears, has a clear view of our future and knows the best route to get there. God is wisdom, and yet so often we seem satisfied to make major decisions without consulting him. What if we put a new twist on Matthew 6:33 and challenged one another to start a "Seek first the kingdom of God" campaign, agreeing to wait on giving out advice until the other has checked with the Lord? A pastor tried this once. When church members asked his counsel on any size issue, he started saying, "How should I know? Why don't you pray and ask God for yourself? He's the one who really knows what's best!" At first people were stunned, and a few got angry that he wouldn't give them an answer. But the longer he stood his ground, the more folks reported that his refusal to help them had deepened their dependence on God and given them better results.

BOOST YOUR OWN WORD POWER

Your words pack a lot of power, so pray about the counsel you give. Weigh what you say with Scripture. And as much as possible, base your advice on the Bible. Save "corrective counsel" for situations in which you've earned the right to speak or have a measure of authority. What you say does make a difference. The advice you offer could affect someone's marriage or career. Start a trend. Agree to give a friend advice, but have him check with God first. Help a new Christian learn to hear God or to use a concordance. Tune up your own spiritual hearing. When you pray, keep your Bible open. Ask God to speak to you through a scripture or write down an impression you get. In serious matters, ask God for several confirmations and listen for the sound of peace reigning in your heart.

Therefore encourage each other with these words.

—1 Thessalonians 4:18

4

CHOICE WORDS OF COURAGE

The Ride of Her Life

I am only one, but I am one. I can't do everything,
but I can do something. And what I can do, I ought to do.
And what I ought to do, by the Grace of God, I shall do.

—EDWARD EVERETT HALE

It was an ordinary Thursday evening in December. And as it often is with historic events, no one in this languid southern town had a clue that one of the brightest spotlights in American history was about to come beaming down upon them. No one could have predicted it would happen here, including the delicate, middle-aged woman who threw the switch.

Rosa had just finished at the downtown Montgomery department store where she worked as a tailor's assistant. She didn't own a car, so like every other night, she walked to the bus stop and waited for the Cleveland Avenue bus to take her home.

When the bus arrived, Rosa climbed on board, paid her fare,

and found a seat. The bus lumbered on, making two or three stops until it ended up in front of the Empire Movie Theater. A new batch of riders filled all the seats until one man, who happened to be white, was left standing in the aisle. The bus driver didn't like this arrangement, so he asked the four black passengers on Rosa's row to move and give the man a seat. Three of them got up. One of them did not. Rosa Parks just sat there.

The driver was perturbed. He saw that a small black woman was still sitting down and wanted to know if she was planning to get up. That's when Rosa spoke the three-word answer that lit the dangling fuse of the entire civil-rights movement: "No, I'm not."[1]

The bus driver warned Rosa that he would have her arrested if she didn't move. "Well, you can do that," was her reply.

Rosa didn't budge, the bus didn't leave, and a few minutes later two policemen arrived in a squad car to cart Rosa to jail.

The situation seemed ridiculous to her. Why should one person give up her seat for another? Shouldn't the seats be first-come, first-served for everyone? She knew her rights as an American, and this bus policy was all wrong.

Rosa hadn't planned to make a point that evening. She was just headed home. But by the following Sunday morning, everyone in all the black churches of Montgomery had heard what she'd done.

That very week, a little known, twenty-six-year-old black man named Martin Luther King, Jr., had come to town. He and other members of the NAACP had been planning to organize a boycott to protest the unfair treatment of blacks on local buses. Rosa's action just moved them ahead of schedule. As a result, Martin

Luther King, Jr., gave a speech that so inspired the blacks of Montgomery that they were willing to walk to work if that's what it took to get needed changes.

And for 381 days, the black men, women, and children of Montgomery, Alabama, staged a peaceful bus protest until the United States Supreme Court finally ruled that the segregation of buses was illegal.

YOU MIGHT LIKE TO KNOW

Rosa Parks is now eighty-seven years old. She and her husband, Raymond, were active members of the local NAACP when she was arrested. She had attended a workshop on civil disobedience the year it happened. She spent only a few hours in jail. With her three words and defiant action, the Reverend Martin Luther King, Jr., was thrust into his calling to become one of the greatest civil-rights leaders of all time.

Rosa is a deaconess for the St. Matthew African Methodist Episcopal Church in Detroit, Michigan. She was named by *Time* magazine as one of the most influential people of the twentieth century. She now receives more than two thousand requests for speeches or endorsements a year, yet she refuses to use her celebrity for profit.[2]

As a child, Rosa endured many racist remarks. During one particularly hurtful encounter, she was seen waving her hand at the white children who taunted her and mumbling "as if possessed by the Holy Spirit." When asked what she was saying, Rosa replied, "I'm praying for them."[3]

The Lone-Star Saint

We need to think about the impact we have on people under and over us.
Probably the greatest gift God has given any of us is
the ability to change lives by our actions or what we say.

—TRUETT CATHY

It doesn't get any hotter than a West Texas oil field in the summertime. But on this particular day, one man may have felt a little more heat than the rest.

We don't really know much about him, not even his first name. Most likely he was a private guy who kept his thoughts to himself and rarely discussed his feelings or faith. But for some reason, on this day, during his lunch hour, the man decided to change all that.

For a while he just waited, leaning against his pickup, eyeing the workers while they wolfed down their lunches. Sweat soaked the hair under his hat and dripped down the back of his neck. Then, when the time felt right, he hitched up his courage and walked toward the crew like a man on a mission.

His workers were a mixed lot: illegal immigrants, drifters, and a few local school kids laying pipe on their summer vacation. And they were suspicious of him, all of them. He was the man, the boss. He told them where to go, what to do, and handed out their paychecks once a week.

But it was lunchtime now. Lunchtime was sacred. They didn't bother him, he didn't bother them, and everyone liked it that way. Except today. Today he was invading their space, coming toward them with a look in his eye that could only mean only one thing: Get back to work.

Or did it?

When the man reached the crew, they had finished eating and had moved on to trading jokes and dealing cards. The boss cleared his throat. A couple of guys looked up.

"Uh, fellows," he said, "I, uh, I just wanted, uh, to invite…I just wanted to tell you that, uh, our church is having a service tonight and, uh…I wanted to invite any of you to come along."

The workers stared at the ground; a few stole snickering glances. What was this? The boss turned preacher? No one looked interested. No one answered him back.

"Well, that's it. Uh, if any of you want to go…uh, let me know."

Then the man sauntered back toward his truck, a two-ton load off his chest. He'd done his part. Now God would have to do the rest.

That afternoon, the crew cracked jokes behind the boss's back. No one joined him for church or said thanks, sir, for asking. And at the end of the day, they hopped in their trucks, gravel flying, in search of the nearest cold beer.

No one accepted his offer, but the man had done his part. And though we can't be sure, it is highly possible that he went on along to the service that night walking a bit taller and just a bit gladder that he had made the effort.

It is now decades later. Summer after scorching summer has fried the air around that West Texas oil field a thousand times. The pipes are still there, though the men that laid them have long since scattered. Who knows where they are?

Well, we do know where one guy is.

He was just a boy that day, a high-school kid, laughing and joking, same as the rest. But he never forgot that boss, the guts he showed and the faith that fueled him. All through high school, the memory of that man's courage lay dormant in the boy, like a seed, undetected. Then in college one day, that seed surfaced again when the tug of God's spirit provoked him to choose.

The choice would cost the kid. He could lose friends, status. It would mean tough changes and a break from his old way of life. But the kid named Max Lucado took the courage he needed to follow God from the man on that West Texas oil field.

These days, Max Lucado can still be found in Texas, pastoring the twenty-five-hundred-member Oak Hills Church in San Antonio. His thirty books have sold more than 11.5 million copies, making him one of the best-selling Christian authors of all time.

In his book *In the Eye of the Storm*, Max wrote an open letter to the nameless oilman who inspired him. It said, "What you did that day wasn't much. And I'm sure you walked away that day thinking that your efforts had been wasted. They weren't.... Thanks for the example. Thanks for the courage. Thanks for giving your lunch to God."[4]

YOU MIGHT LIKE TO KNOW

Max Lucado was the youngest of four children. His mother worked as nurse, and his father was an oil-field mechanic. He grew up attending the Church of Christ but spent much of his teen years "drinking and partying and totally disinterested in spiritual matters."[5] After committing his life to Christ in college, Max got a master's degree in biblical studies and then worked as a missionary in Brazil for five years.

Max emphasizes that he is a minister first and a writer second. His books are drawn from his sermons. Outside his church, Max receives more than a thousand offers to speak each year. But in 1999, he accepted only two. A Max Lucado title has appeared on the Christian Booksellers Association hardcover bestseller list every month for the last seven years. Max is the only author to win the Gold Medallion Christian Book of the Year three times.

∞

The White Flag of Courage

Two-thirds of help is to give courage.
—IRISH PROVERB

At a key point during the Civil War, just before General Sherman launched his famous march to the sea, the Confederate army had maneuvered itself into an advantageous position near Altoona Pass. Fifteen hundred Union soldiers were stationed at Altoona to protect more than a million rations and other valuable supplies. But their numbers were no match for the six thousand Confederate soldiers who had them completely surrounded.

Union General Corse was in command at this post, and though he was obviously outflanked, the general refused to surrender. A fierce battle broke out. Before long, Corse and his soldiers were driven back into a small fort at the top of a hill.

To prolong the fight seemed fruitless. Many Union men had been killed or wounded. General Corse had been shot in the head three times, and his second-in-command was fighting wounded. The Confederates were calling for surrender.

But then something happened.

Off in the distance, some twenty miles away, one of the Union officers spied a white flag waving on top of Kenesaw Mountain. The flag was sending a signal. And for a few minutes, signals bounced from the hill to the mountain and back. Then the officer carried the message to his commander. The message said, "Hold the fort; I am coming. W. T. Sherman."

A cheer went up among the Union men. With renewed hope, they continued to fight. More than half of the men in their unit were killed or wounded in the battle, but the Union soldiers valiantly held the fort for three more hours until an advance guard from Sherman's army finally arrived.

The Confederates were forced to retreat. And the Union soldiers were saved.

Far outnumbered in an impossible fight, the fort was doomed. The men should have all died or, at best, been captured. But six words of courage from a general they believed in packed all the promise they needed to prevail.

Six years later, in 1870, this account was repeated at a Sunday-school meeting in Rockford, Illinois, attended by the great hymn writer Philip Bliss. He was moved by the story and instantly got an idea for a song.

The next day, as Bliss was leading the singing at a YMCA meeting in Chicago, he walked to the chalkboard and wrote the words to a brand-new hymn. After singing three verses of the song, Bliss turned to the audience and asked them to join him as the first to sing what would become one of his most famous hymns: "Hold the Fort." The first verse and chorus read, "Ho! My comrades, see the signal waving in the sky! Reinforcements now appearing, victory is nigh. 'Hold the fort, for I am coming,' Jesus signals still; wave the answer back to heaven, 'By thy grace we will.'"[6]

The hymn quickly grew in popularity and was soon sung all over the world.

In 1873, D. L. Moody and his song leader, Ira Sankey, introduced "Hold the Fort" at their famous revival meetings in Great

Britain. One of the sponsors of the meetings, Lord Shaftesbury, was so inspired by the hymn that at their last meeting he announced, "If Mr. Sankey has done no more than teach the people to sing 'Hold the Fort,' he has conferred an inestimable blessing on the British Empire."[7]

No doubt, years later, during the dark days of World War II, another generation of British Christians felt much the same comfort singing "Hold the Fort" as Union soldiers did when they received that message.

YOU MIGHT LIKE TO KNOW

General Sherman flew his white signal flag from a pine tree atop Kenesaw Mountain. Years after the war, the tree was cut down and made into celebratory souvenirs—one of which was a conducting baton given to D. L. Moody's music director, Ira Sankey. P. P. Bliss thought he had written better songs than "Hold the Fort" and did not want to be remembered solely for it. But his burial monument in Pennsylvania reads, "P. P. Bliss, author of 'Hold the Fort.'" Bliss also wrote the music for the classic hymn "It Is Well with My Soul."

∞

Evangelism Implosion

Real encouragement occurs when words are spoken from a heart of love to another's recognized fear.

—LARRY CRABB

Jim was fresh out of seminary, ready to take on the world, but the forty-five members of his fledgling church weren't so sure he could do it. Week after week, he gave them the best sermons money could buy, words from Spurgeon and Luther and Calvin. He meant well. His heart was right. But after ten and a half months, his congregation had dwindled to seventeen people.

Maybe it was the fact that they didn't have their own building. Or maybe it was the fact that this was South Florida, and they were stuck in an un-air-conditioned school cafeteria every Sunday. Jim wasn't totally sure, but he knew he had to do something. If "the mountain wouldn't come to Muhammad," he quoted, "then Muhammad would go to the mountain."

Now, church visitation was not on Jim's list of fun things to do. He was a fairly shy person. But he was also desperate. So he braced himself, grabbed some visitors' cards, and drove to the first person's home.

When he knocked on the door, he expected a sweet little gray-haired woman to open it. But instead, a huge hulk of a man stood in front of him, clutching a can of beer, wearing an undershirt, and smoking a cigar.

Jim announced that he had come to see the man's mother and was secretly relieved when he found out she wasn't home. But as he turned to leave, the son invited him inside. Slightly intimidated, Jim was obliged to accept.

Once inside, the conversation bounced around from sports to the weather. And the layman who accompanied Jim was getting impatient. He knew they hadn't come for small talk. Weren't they on kingdom business? But the novice pastor's behavior was like a plane circling the runway with its landing gear broken.

The visit that night went nowhere. Dejected and disappointed, Jim prayed, "Lord, what am I doing here? Surely this is all a big mistake. You didn't call me into the ministry to miserably fail."

About that same time, a letter came inviting Jim to lead a ten-day evangelistic meeting in Atlanta. It seemed like a cruel joke for God to play on him, but he picked out some sermons and headed up north, happy to leave the headaches of his new church venture.

When Jim got to Atlanta, he was greeted with the news that he would be preaching every night. This thrilled him. Preaching he could handle. Then the man organizing the meeting said, "However, that's not the most important thing."

Jim thought to himself, *Oh, Lord, don't let this guy say what I think he's going to say next. He looks like "that type."*

The man proceeded to tell Jim that they would be going door to door every morning and afternoon and even sometimes at night after the services. He told Jim he would have the opportunity to witness to people "eyeball to eyeball and toenail to toenail" and that he had "saved all the really tough nuts" for him.

This was not good. Jim was billed as a great evangelist, but he didn't know the first thing about evangelism.

The next morning, Jim and the local preacher went to the first home on their list, and another very large man answered the door. Again they covered the news, sports, and weather. Then about the time Jim was ready to leave, the preacher interrupted and said, "Well, Hank, I brought this professional preacher out here to talk to you about your soul."

With much fear and trembling, Jim jumped in and in no time had Hank fighting mad. Then something from Jim's Systematic Theology 302B class occurred to him. Maybe Hank was so resistant because he was not one of God's "elect."

But the preacher with Jim thought differently. Within fifteen minutes, he had turned the conversation around, and Hank was on his knees. And during the next few days, fifty-four people came forward; most of them had been led to Christ in their homes that week by that hometown preacher.

At the close of the meetings, Jim asked the preacher, "How in the world did you ever learn to do this?"

"It was in this very same evangelistic crusade last year. We really had an evangelist. He took me out with him, and I learned from watching him."

"Well, I learned from watching him." Those words stuck with Jim, and soon he was witnessing everywhere he went, just like the Atlanta preacher had showed him.

A year later, back in Fort Lauderdale, tired and worn out from doing all the work himself, Jim got an idea: What if he taught his own laymen to witness alongside him? One by one, he began taking people from his church out visiting. Then when they got the hang of it, they would split off, taking others with them. It was then, in 1962, that Dr. D. James Kennedy of Coral Ridge Presbyterian Church began to notice the scriptural pattern and said, "Lord, this is it. This is the way." And from that discovery, the astonishingly successful Evangelism Explosion lay-witnessing program was born.[8]

YOU MIGHT LIKE TO KNOW

Evangelism Explosion International is the first ministry to be established in every nation on earth. Dr. Kennedy committed his life to Christ after being awakened one morning to the voice of a stern radio preacher who said, "Suppose you were to die today and stand before God, and he were to ask you, 'What right do you have to enter into my heaven?' What would you say?"

For fifteen years, Dr. Kennedy's church was the fastest-growing Presbyterian church in America. His television program, *The Coral Ridge Hour*, is broadcast from his ninety-five-hundred-member church to thirty-five thousand cities and towns across the United States. And his radio program, *Truths That Transform*, is broadcast on more than twelve hundred television and radio outlets nation-wide. He is Chancellor of Knox Theological Seminary; Founder of the Center for Christian Statesmanship in Washington, D.C., and of the Center for Reclaiming America. He is the author of more than forty books.

THE COURAGEOUS WORD OF GOD

*During the fourth watch of the night Jesus went out to them,
walking on the lake. When the disciples saw him walking on the lake,
they were terrified. "It's a ghost," they said, and cried out in fear.
But Jesus immediately said to them: "Take courage! It is I. Don't be afraid."*
—MATTHEW 14:25–27

Because it arrives at an odd or seemingly ill-timed moment, our first reaction to the unusual is often fear. We are quick to jump to the conclusion that anything outrageous, challenging, or out of the ordinary could not possibly be of God and is most likely from the devil. We long to be full of faith, but like the disciples, we are often frightened and superstitious in the face of the supernatural. How often has Christ appeared to us and, instead of seeing his glory, we have cried, "Ghost!"? How often has he visited us in the midst of something new or difficult and we have buried our heads in the sand, afraid to join him in it? There is comfort in the fact that even those closest to Jesus didn't always recognize him on the first pass. And there is solace in the knowledge that he is sensitive to our misjudgments and reassuring in our unbelief.

He could come any day, walking on our lake, cruising by our boat, daring us to trust that it is he. Christ knows that we'll need help to follow him. He knows that we'll need words to obey. That's why he calls to our cringing hearts, "Take courage! It is I. Don't be afraid."

BOOST YOUR OWN WORD POWER

Write a note to someone who is struggling. Include some courage from God. Recount for them God's faithfulness. Review for them his power. Give them a story from your own life. Build up their confidence in Christ. Read Scripture aloud or over the phone to someone who has been given bad news.

Consider this: If you were to die tonight, what would your last words be? Write them down, stick them in your Bible, or share them with a friend. Invite a coworker to join you at church. Talk more openly about your faith. And if you feel fearful, write out your testimony and memorize it or even print it in brochure form. Commit to the next evangelism-training course your church offers. Pray for more boldness. Be strong and courageous. And leave the results to God.

The words of the wise are like goads.

—ECCLESIASTES 12:11

5

CHOICE WORDS OF CORRECTION

The Long Arm of God's Love

God rarely allows a soul to see how great a blessing he is.
—OSWALD CHAMBERS

It wasn't the first time a young man who was sweet in high school went sour after graduation. Dawson had been a leader in school; he was the student-body president, captain of the basketball team, and even the senior-class valedictorian, whose speech at commencement was titled "Morality versus Legality." But Dawson had been living a double life, and after getting drunk one night, he concluded that it was just too hard to be holy.

Dawson tried to straighten up, but the dark side had a hold on him. Among other things, he was a prolific liar. His mother often told people she couldn't believe a word he said. Sure, he felt guilty. He even tried to break the habit by scraping his knuckles on a brick wall. But lying was so ingrained in him that his self-punishments never worked for long.

Stealing and gambling were also big problems. As a child, he regularly stole money from his mother's purse, which later led to stealing from the school locker fund. And eventually, Dawson's gambling got so out of hand that his boss threatened to fire him if he ever brought dice on the job again.

After high school, Dawson gave up all pretense of virtue and spent the next three years drinking on the beach, stunt driving his red Buick, gambling at pool and dice games, and meeting girls in dance halls.

When folks who had known him in better days passed him on the street, Dawson ignored them. He had completely changed. And every night he came home late so that his sickly mother wouldn't nag him about his lifestyle.

Then one night, Dawson was arrested at a local amusement area. He was too drunk to find his car. When the policeman took his keys, all Dawson could think of was his mother saying, "Son, if I ever hear you are in jail, I'll die."

Dawson didn't want to hurt his mother, but the words and actions of the policeman that night had an even greater impact on him. The cop was a big man who talked to Dawson like a father. He sat him down and asked, "Son, do you like this kind of life?"

Dawson answered, "Sir, I hate it."

The policeman must have believed him. He didn't take Dawson to jail but left him on the bench to sober up. Three hours later, the policeman returned the young man's car keys in exchange for a promise to change.

Somehow Dawson's mother found out about his brush with the law, and she phoned a friend named Cora and asked her to pray for him. The next day, Cora called back and reported that she and some other women had spent the night praying. She said, "The Lord showed me a vision of Dawson holding a Bible, speaking to a large group of people, and the burden has lifted. Don't worry about Dawson anymore."[1]

Miraculously, Dawson did end up holding a Bible and speaking to large groups of people. In fact, that very picture would be repeated hundreds and hundreds of times.

After his encounter with the policeman, Dawson returned to church and, thanks to his competitive nature, began memorizing Scripture to win a youth-group contest. It was the memorization of scripture that finally led Dawson Trotman to Christ. Years later, those very scriptures became the cornerstone of the worldwide ministry he founded called the Navigators.

Soon after his conversion, Dawson taught high-school students and Sunday-school classes. Later God led him to disciple Christian sailors using his well-known "wheel" diagram, which proposed a balanced approach to the Christian life with prayer, Bible study, evangelism, and fellowship as spokes on the wheel. By the end of World War II, thousands of Christians on ships and at bases around the world were trained to multiply their lives by discipling other believers.

The legacy of Dawson Trotman is only explainable in God-terms.

One sunny June day in 1956, Dawson drowned while trying to save a floundering swimmer at a lake in the Adirondacks. He was fifty years old. At the time of his death, he had personally discipled hundreds of men, his organization had a modest staff of 140 in the U.S. and overseas, and he had written the systematic follow-up materials used by the Billy Graham Evangelistic Association for its crusades.

Dawson Trotman died young, but the multiplication principle he so passionately modeled lives on.

Today thousands of churches and other ministries have incorporated many of Dawson's principles and materials. The Navigators is now a multifaceted, worldwide ministry with branches that include book and magazine publications (NavPress), student ministry (NavYouth and Eagle Lake Camps), military ministry, collegiate ministry, the Glen Eyrie Conference Center, and church discipleship ministries, just to name a few. The U.S. International Ministry Group, a missions branch of the Navigators, currently serves 460 long-term American staff members in sixty-five countries.[2]

And it all began from a seed, the seed of the Word of God that was planted after a California policeman cared enough to confront a miserable, drunken kid about the direction of his life.

YOU MIGHT LIKE TO KNOW

In Billy Graham's message at Dawson Trotman's funeral, he said, "Dawson loved the Word of God. I think more than anybody else he taught me to love it.... Dawson was a man with a vision.... No project was too big to tackle if he felt God was in it.... To Dawson, God was big, and the world was little.... I remember in London, Dawson would slip into my little room when things would seem impossible, and we'd get down on our knees and pray."[3] The Navigators is headquartered in a castle called Glen Eyrie in Colorado Springs, Colorado.

Revenge of the High-School Math Teacher

*The dreams begin with a teacher who believes in you,
who tugs and pushes and leads you on to the next plateau,
sometimes poking you with a sharp stick called truth.*

—DAN RATHER

Kevin was every teacher's worst nightmare. He had a knack for clowning around that went beyond the normal, expected antics of most high-school boys. When he walked into class at the start of a new term, everyone grinned and nudged each other. They knew from experience that if Kevin's name was on the roll, their class would be a riot.

It seemed that Kevin's main goal in life was to get attention. And at an early age, he had discovered that the best way to get attention was to do something outrageous.

One night, as the eight-year-old mascot at a high-school basketball game, Kevin spotted the opposing team's mascot dressed up in a tiger suit. Suddenly the idea came to him to yank off the tiger's tail. In a flash, he scampered across the gym and made his heist. That stunt won him banner headlines in the next school newspaper and fueled his jets for even more tricks.

In high school, Kevin was known for crawling out of class on his hands and knees and setting trash cans on fire. Once he even talked the whole school into putting alarm clocks in their lockers and setting them to go off at 2:00 P.M.

Scholarship was *not* Kevin's forte. In his senior year, he gave his math teacher such a hard time that she resigned from teaching. With graduation just months away, Kevin, who had been failing math, was assigned to another teacher who tutored him after school in her own home. Her name was Eleanor Wilson, and she was neither distressed nor impressed with Kevin's rowdy reputation.

One day when Mrs. Wilson saw Kevin in the hall, she pulled him aside, looked him straight in the eye, and asked, "Kevin, when are you going to stop playing your game?"

"What game is that, Teach?"

"The game that you play best," she smiled. "Being the worst!"

At the time, Kevin laughed and tried to slough off the comment. But somehow her words rang true, and at odd times for the rest of his life, he would still hear her speaking them.

Soon after this encounter, Kevin sought to channel the abundance of his negative energy in a more positive direction. He went in to see the school guidance counselor and said, "I've been doing some heavy thinking, and I want to go to college." But the counselor just looked up through his glasses and remarked, "With your record, I couldn't get you admitted to reform school."

Kevin had lost valuable time and was ill-prepared for higher education. By his last semester, he ranked fourth from the bottom of his class. But he was determined to get into college. He applied to 160 schools and was turned down by every one of them. Finally, after receiving letters from his older brother and his pastor, North Park College in Chicago agreed to enroll him—but only on probation.

Kevin didn't last long at North Park. By his second year, he was failing classes and reverting to pranks. And when he and a roommate were caught raiding the conscience fund of the college ice-cream machine, the dean firmly showed him the exit.

With this setback, Kevin was forced to move out west with his parents and enter the world of work, which he had been desperately hoping to avoid. He had no skills or training, so he got a job as a janitor, making $195 a month.

It wasn't long before Kevin figured out that the janitor job was going nowhere. Convinced he was made for better things, Kevin tried college again, this time enrolling in a night course at the University of Arizona. But he flunked that too.

Then one day while he was emptying a trash can, Kevin spied an attractive girl coming down the hall. She was a nurse's aide in the building where he worked. He brashly waltzed up to her and asked, "How would you like to go to the New York World's Fair with me?" The girl turned him down for the fair but agreed to lunch at McDonald's. It was this girl, Sande (who later became his wife), who encouraged Kevin to explore a relationship with Jesus Christ. And when he did, the downward spiral of his life took a definite turn upward.

Kevin went back to the University of Arizona and took another course. This time, he made the highest grade in a class of six hundred. After that, he went on to get his undergraduate, master's, and doctoral degrees, managing to stay on the dean's list for most of that time.

During those years, Kevin often thought of Mrs. Wilson and her belief in him. Her corrective encouragement—plus a comment made by Sande's supervisor, who said, "Don't associate with that janitor; he'll never amount to anything"[4]—kept him motivated toward success.

Today, the kid who was either emptying trash cans or setting them on fire is now internationally known Christian psychologist and conference speaker Dr. Kevin Leman. He is the consulting psychologist for *Good Morning America* and has authored more than seventeen books, including *The New Birth Order Book, Sex Begins in the Kitchen,* and *Becoming a Couple of Promise.*

Amazingly, God used the stern but loving words of a wise teacher to turn a disorderly young schoolboy into a dedicated

Christian leader who would one day write a best-selling book called *Making Your Children Mind without Losing Yours*.

YOU MIGHT LIKE TO KNOW

Dr. Kevin Leman held the post of assistant dean of students at the University of Arizona for eleven years. He has been a guest on *Oprah, Larry King Live, CBS Good Morning,* and *The Today Show* as well as the *Focus on the Family* radio program with Dr. James Dobson. Dr. Leman also hosts a radio program, *Parent Talk,* with Randy Carlson.

Several years ago, Dr. Leman visited his former math teacher, Mrs. Wilson, to thank her for the challenge she gave him in those closing weeks of high school. She smiled and humbly said, "Oh, I did very little, Kevin. You did it yourself. You were a challenge, all right, but I knew you could do it if you wanted to!"

Other words that highly impacted Dr. Leman came in 1981 from fellow psychologist and author James Dobson. The two were having lunch in Arcadia, California, and Dr. Leman asked Dr. Dobson to give him one good piece of advice for his life. Dobson thought a minute then said, "Just run everything by [your wife] first."

$$\infty$$

The Coach Who Tackled the Church Boy

I dare you to be the strongest boy in the class.
—WILLIAM H. DANFORTH'S TEACHER

As Coach Pulliman eyed the roster for his Chattanooga Howard High School football team, he took a long, hard look at number seventy-seven. He knew talent when he saw it, and this boy, Reggie, had a truckload. But Reggie had an attitude problem, and the coach knew that if he didn't tackle it soon, all the kid's potential would go to waste.

According to Coach Pulliman, Reggie's "problem" was that he was just a "nice, big Sunday-school boy, who didn't want to hurt anybody," not exactly the mind-set he required on the football field. So the coach devised a plan to toughen Reggie up, to make him the kind of player who could take the punishment necessary to perform at the college and maybe even professional level.

After practice one day, the coach called Reggie over and said, "Let me tell you something, Reggie. I really believe that you could be the best defensive player ever to play the game of football." Becoming a professional football player was one of Reggie's life goals, and hearing these words only fueled his desire to work harder for his coach.

But Reggie soon found out that his idea of hard work and the coach's were leagues apart.

From the day he spoke those words, the coach began playing rough with Reggie. Sometimes he would push Reggie and harass him on the field or in the gym. Reggie thought the coach had turned on him and was confused by his change in behavior.

There were times the coach caught him off-guard in the gym and challenged him to wrestle. But if Reggie got out of a hold, one of the other coaches would throw him back down, and coach Pulliman would go after him again. Sometimes the coach pushed him to the point of tears and then laughed and called him a crybaby. This cruel treatment incensed Reggie. He had a reputation for being a cool guy, and he hated the embarrassment this brought him in front of his friends.

But Coach Pulliman was relentless. Day after day, he hounded his player. Once, in a basketball game, the six-foot-two-inch, 260-pound coach jumped in to guard Reggie.

The coach continually fouled him. Finally he elbowed Reggie so hard in the chest that he slammed down the basketball and walked off the court crying.

Reggie's friends tried to comfort him, but he shrugged them off, yelling, "He wrestles me, he punches me, he makes me cry, and I'm getting sick of it!" Storming into the locker room, Reggie sat on a bench, tears staining his face.

A few minutes later, the coach walked in. Reggie expected an apology from him, but instead, the coach got down in front of him, grabbed the front of his shirt, and said, "If you think I'm gonna apologize, you might as well go in there and get ready for your next whipping. Until you start fighting me back, I'm gonna keep kicking your butt."

That did it. His words set Reggie on fire. They made him so angry that every chance he got, he went after the coach with every ounce of his strength.

From that moment, whenever they played basketball and the coach shoved him, Reggie shoved him back, even harder. When the coach wrestled and pinned him down, Reggie would fight back until the day came that he finally beat him. When that happened, the coach taunted Reggie in front of the other players and demanded a rematch. But Reggie said, "Look, Coach, I don't gotta give you nothing! I've got the championship now, and I ain't gonna give it up just to give you another chance." But the coach did get a second chance, and Reggie beat him again. And from then on, according to Coach Pulliman, Reggie White was "a holy terror."

It was years before Reggie discovered that the coach's relentless pounding was part of a plan he had devised to build toughness and confidence in him. The coach knew that if Reggie were going to make it in collegiate and professional football he would need "the hide of a rhinoceros."

Today Coach Pulliman's words and workouts seem harsh and abusive, but they pushed Reggie White to the top of his game.

By his senior year at Chattanooga Howard High School, Reggie was named All-State in basketball and All-American in football, as well as football and basketball player of the year in the city of Chattanooga. That year he also received the national Two-Sport Player of the Year award, with soon-to-be NBA basketball legend Patrick Ewing coming in as runner-up.

Years later, Reggie called Coach Pulliman to thank him for the "star treatment" he received under his mentorship. The coach laughed and for the first time admitted, "I called the parents of all you guys and asked if I could do to them what I did to you. I asked your mother and all the other parents if I could be really hard on all you guys in order to build your confidence—and your mother was the only one who said yes."

Reggie received offers to play football for Alabama, UCLA, Michigan, Miami, Oklahoma, and Ohio State, but he chose the University of Tennessee, the school Coach Pulliman played for in college.

Reggie later recalled, "My first day of college football, I absorbed more physical punishment and verbal abuse than in a month of high-school football." And after being carried off the practice field on a stretcher, Reggie called his mother to say that he was giving up football.

But his mother, reminding him of a promise he had made, said, "Reggie, remember what you told me before you left home? You told me, 'As long as God blesses me with the ability to play football, I'm gonna give it everything I've got and I'm never gonna give up!'"

Reggie stayed on to play football for the Tennessee Volunteers. His senior year, he was Southeastern Conference Player of the Year, a finalist for the Lombardi Trophy, and a consensus All-American. But if he hadn't accepted his high-school coach's tough correction, Reggie White might never have stuck it out and become known as one the toughest guys in the National Football League.

As a professional football player with the Philadelphia Eagles, Reggie was voted All-NFL seven times. In 1993, he signed as a free agent with the Green Bay Packers and played a deciding role in their 1997 Super-Bowl victory. Then in 1999, Reggie White, the "nice little church boy" from Chattanooga, retired as arguably the best defensive end in professional football history, with the impressive distinction of being the all-time NFL leader in quarterback sacks at 192.

Reggie White once said, "Good coaches, the ones who have a lasting impact on your life, are people you remember as long as you live. The lessons they teach you become part of the fiber of your being, and for years afterward, you can remember their names, their faces and the sound of their voices because they had such a deep and powerful impact on your life."[5]

YOU MIGHT LIKE TO KNOW

When Reggie was thirteen, he made a personal commitment to Jesus Christ. He was so zealous about his relationship with God that he carried his Bible to school every day and pointed to certain passages whenever he caught other kids doing wrong. At age seventeen, he became a licensed minister and preached his first sermon to a group of ministers at St. John's Baptist Church. He is most recently known for speaking out on the spiritual and moral climate of our day and for funding church and inner-city projects for young entrepreneurs. He is also the founder of his own record label, Big Doggie Records, which he created to promote positive music for young people.

A Failure to Communicate

The people who influence us are those who
have stood unconsciously for the right thing; they are like the stars
and the lilies; and the joy of God flows through them.

—OSWALD CHAMBERS

One night in early spring, a medical student named Wilfred Grenfell was on his way home from seeing patients when he noticed a crowd gathering down the street. Curiosity got the best of him, so he slipped in the back of a lecture hall only to discover he had stumbled upon a large religious meeting.

Wilfred was familiar with church affairs; his father was an ordained Anglican priest. But this particular meeting seemed quite different from the services he was used to attending.

Wilfred was born into an upper-class British family and was accustomed to the best of everything. His father was the headmaster of an upscale preparatory school, and his mother was the daughter of a high-ranking British army officer. Wilfred had attended the elite Marlborough School and then went on to study at Queen's College, Oxford.

This particular night, as Wilfred dropped in on the meeting, a man was praying at the front. It was evident to Wilfred that the man's words lacked sincerity. As the prayer droned on in a dry, pious monotone, Wilfred decided to leave. But just as he turned to go, a spirited man on the platform jumped up and shouted, "Let us have a hymn while our brother finishes his prayer!"[6]

Wilfred was shocked and somewhat amused. Later he said, "Unconventionality, common sense, or humor in anything 'religious' was new to me. Brawling or disturbing the order of ritual is criminal in the Established Church."

The young medical student was an agnostic who was not the least bit interested in God. But after this incident, he leaned over to the person next to him and asked about this unconventional man. Wilfred learned that the man was the keynote speaker for the evening. The speaker's boisterous comment so intrigued him that he decided to stay and see what else might happen.

Wilfred didn't know it at the time, but the speaker that evening was none other than the famous American evangelist D. L. Moody.

Wilfred sat spellbound as Moody masterfully spun captivating, true-life tales. The young man was drawn to the simple message of the gospel and the bold, compelling man who proclaimed it. As Moody concluded his message, Wilfred felt as if the preacher had appealed directly to him when he asked, "Why don't you turn your life over to Christ? He can do more with it than you can."[7]

After the meeting, Wilfred picked up a little booklet called *How to Read the Bible* and, in the weeks ahead, faithfully followed its directions. He studied large portions of Scripture and eventually committed his life to serving Christ as a medical missionary.

Soon after this, Wilfred heard that a missionary organization called the Royal National Mission to Deep Sea Fishermen needed a doctor aboard their mercy ship. He had always loved the sea, so he jumped at the chance to serve there. But the ship was merely a stopover on the way to Wilfred's ultimate destination.

In 1892, he visited the rugged coast of Labrador. There he saw hungry, struggling people who barely survived along the dreary shoreline and discovered that there was not one doctor in the whole country. Wilfred's heart went out to them. Amid protests from his mission agency, he decided that he would make the people of Labrador his life's work.

Once on his mission field, Wilfred often risked his life as he piloted his launch around jagged cliffs, shifting currents, and blasting winds. Perhaps his most memorable moment came as he raced a dog-sled team across an icy bay. He knew the trip was risky since the spring thaw had already started, but a young boy's life was at stake, so he drove the dogs across the frozen bay. The ice didn't hold. Suddenly he, the dogs, and the sled plunged into the frigid water. Wilfred saved himself and the dogs by climbing onto a large patch of ice, but as temperatures fell, he was forced to kill the animals and to wrap himself in their bloody skins in order to survive. The next morning, as Wilfred was near death, a group of men discovered him. At risk to their own lives, they navigated the icy waters, rescuing the doctor they had come to love.

To raise funds for his mission, Wilfred traveled across America, telling the tales of his adventurous life. As he preached he said, "Following Christ has given me more fun and adventure than any other kind of life.... When two courses are open, follow the most venturesome."[8] This struck a chord with audiences, because everywhere he went, "Grenfell Societies" sprang up. Many young men and women were so impressed by Wilfred's sacrifice that they left home to join his work.

Thanks to the humorous, unorthodox statement of D. L. Moody, Wilfred Grenfell, once a wealthy young medical student, was compelled to Christ and spent forty years ministering among the people of Labrador.

Moody could not have known that his off-the-cuff commentary of a pious man's prayer would be used by God to save thousands of destitute lives. No doubt his only hope in that moment was just to save his meeting.

YOU MIGHT LIKE TO KNOW

Wilfred Grenfell was responsible for building hospitals and clinics and attending to evangelism and discipleship among the Eskimo, Indian, and white population of Labrador. In 1927, he was knighted for his forty years of service and received an honorary doctorate from St. Andrews University. After that night in the lecture hall, it was fourteen years before Wilfred Grenfell saw D. L. Moody again. Of serving others, Grenfell once said, "The service we render others is the rent we pay for our room on earth."[9]

∞

The Wife Who Had More Than Enough

Find out how much God has given you and from it take what you need, the remainder is needed by others.

—AUGUSTINE

Linda had had it. She was fed up with her husband's money-grabbing workaholism and extravagant lifestyle. She was tired of his get-rich-quick schemes and expensive toys. So one day she packed her bags and headed for New York.

It was true that Millard had a knack for making money; he'd been working at it since he was six. That's when his father gave him a pig to raise. By the time he was twelve, he had added rabbits, chickens, and cattle to his portfolio. It seemed everything he touched turned to money.

Millard grew up going to church with his family. He knew the Bible said that it was difficult for a rich man to enter the kingdom of God, but he was up for the challenge. His goal was to be a Christian rich man, since he had heard that all things were possible with God.

In college, Millard and a friend paid their way through the University of Alabama by selling directories, birthday cakes, and desk blotters. They invested their profits in rental apartments for students. By graduation, they were making $50,000 a year.

After finishing law school, Millard and his partner went into the mail-order business. But his big money came later—selling fund-raising cookbooks to the Future Homemakers of America and other groups.

By the time Millard was twenty-nine, he had become a millionaire and made it his mission to increase his earnings tenfold. He had given Linda all the money she needed and more. They had a full-time maid, a new Lincoln Continental, a cabin at the lake, as well as cattle, horses, and lakes stocked with fish. But Linda wasn't happy. Her husband was married to his money, not to her. That's when she announced that she was going to New York to think about the future of their marriage.

"I was in agony," Millard said. "Never before...had I suffered as I did during those days. Everything else—business, sales, profits, prestige, everything that had seemed so important—paled into total meaninglessness. I began to examine my life and to ask what it was all about. [I imagined God asking me] what I had done with my life. I could hear myself squeaking, 'Lord, I sold...a lot of cookbooks.' In the presence of God that sounded so ridiculous I could only cringe."[10]

Linda's exit was not a part of Millard's plan. It stopped him dead in his tracks. He deeply loved his wife, so he went to her seeking reconciliation.

In a tearful meeting in New York City, Millard and Linda were reunited. Then they sold their business, gave the money to charities, and went on a mission trip to Africa, touring schools, hospitals, and refugee programs.

When they returned, they lived, worked, and studied the Bible on a communal farm in Americus, Georgia. And it was there that Millard and Linda Fuller, along with Clarence Jordan, first developed the concepts of a house building venture that eventually resulted in the formation of Habitat for Humanity, now the largest nonprofit housing organization in the United States.

It seemed that any business Millard Fuller touched would have succeeded. But God had other ideas, bigger ideas than even Millard could imagine. And the more than four hundred thousand people worldwide who have been helped into a new home are extremely grateful he did.

YOU MIGHT LIKE TO KNOW

Habitat for Humanity International is a nonprofit, ecumenical Christian housing ministry. On the purpose of his ministry, Millard Fuller said, "What Habitat does is much more than sheltering people. It's what it does for people on the inside. It's that intangible quality of hope. Many people without decent housing consider themselves life's losers. A Habitat house is the first victory they may have ever had. And it changes them."[11]

Millard and Linda Fuller choose not to air-condition their home to save the expense. In 1997, Fuller refused to increase his forty-four-thousand-dollar salary, though the annual budget for Habitat for Humanity International was seventy-eight million dollars. HFHI is one of America's most popular charities.[12] Habitat for Humanity homeowners must help build, pay for, and maintain the homes they are given in order to qualify for them. For more than fourteen years, former president Jimmy Carter has sponsored an annual Habitat work camp with up to fourteen thousand volunteers joining him.[13]

Fuller has written seven books, including *Theology of the Hammer, No More Shacks!*, and his latest, *More Than Houses*.

HEEDING GOD'S WORD OF CORRECTION

*A dispute arose among them as to which of them was
considered to be greatest. Jesus said to them,
"The kings of the Gentiles lord it over them.... But you are not to be like
that. Instead, the greatest among you should be like the youngest."*
—LUKE 22:24–26

In the natural world, we are taught to think that skyscraping stature is the crowning prize of life. But then Christ comes along and throws a kink in our thinking. He corrects our assumptions of superiority by leading us step by step, all the way back to the bottom of the ladder of success. He invites us to join him in servant lifestyle and reminds us to study the young. Maybe when he said that "the greatest among you should be like the youngest," he was thinking of young David or Joseph. In the beginning, both David and Joseph were runts of the bunch. Both were given menial tasks and lorded over by their brothers. Yet both willingly submitted to God's secret of servanthood, and then, after graduating from the boot camp of humility, both rose to unprecedented greatness.

Our culture is consumed with position and advancement, but to those with his family name, Jesus says, "You are not to be like that."

As we speed off to leave our mark on the world, Christ calmly steps onto the track and waves a yellow caution flag. He tells us again that it is not the one racing his engine in the lead pole position who wins his praise. More likely, it is the one willing to serve hot dogs in the stands who pleases him most.

BOOST YOUR OWN WORD POWER

Sharpen your spiritual senses. Keep on the lookout for God's leadings, and be willing to follow through with the assignment he gives, even those occasions that seem to be leading nowhere. He is the message. You are simply the messenger. Avoid speaking your own mind, but seek God's will in every situation, acting as his spokesperson at a moment's notice. Be cautious in your corrections. Think of the words that the Lord has used to admonish you, and train your tongue to his truths. Remember, it is God's kindness that leads us to repentance.

The tongue has the power of life.

—PROVERBS 18:21

6

CHOICE WORDS OF CONVERSION

A Mysterious Moment of Truth

Kind words are the music of the world.
They have a power that seems to be beyond natural causes, as though they
were some angel's song which had lost its way and come back to earth.

—ANONYMOUS

How many thousands of mothers through the centuries have wondered if their prayers for their wayward children would be answered? Monica was one of those mothers. She had already spent thirty years on her knees and still saw no change in her son.

Monica was a devoted Christian mother and taught her son, Aurelius, all she knew about Christ. And through the years, the boy witnessed her dedication and devout life. But as it was for many young men in the third century, Aurelius was sent away at the age of fifteen to broaden his education, and his mother's influence soon faded.

Aurelius was a brilliant student. He studied law, rhetoric, and philosophy and quickly mastered all his subjects. But during this time other things began to master him. His lifestyle grew loose and promiscuous. He fell in love with a girl, and they lived together but never married. Before long, she was pregnant with his son.

Searching for knowledge and intellectual achievement, Aurelius was drawn to the great cities of his day. He searched for mentors who could challenge him, studied the works of Cicero, and adopted the teachings of Manicheanism.

For years, his mother prayed for him and begged him to read the Bible in order to gain a more spiritual world-view. But the times Aurelius appeased her, he got nothing from the Scriptures; for him, the books of Aristotle were more inspiring.

Monica grieved for her son's soul. And after sobbing her concern to a priest, he comforted her by saying, "It cannot be that the son of these tears should be lost."[1]

Eventually Aurelius wrote books of his own and gathered a group of disciples who lived and traveled with him. One of their trips took them to Milan, where Aurelius became acquainted with a bishop named Ambrose. The bishop was renowned for his persuasive oratory skills—the very skills Aurelius wanted to learn. So he began to spend time with the man, hoping to learn his oratory secrets. And as time went by, many aspects of the bishop's Christian teaching began to influence him.

But in his personal life, Aurelius was in a moral crisis. His inability to control his sexual desires depressed him. So he began reading the Bible and regularly listening to the bishop. He enjoyed the hymns and chants in the church services, but his moral failures tormented him. Much of what he had learned contained high ideals, and it distressed him that he could not live up to these ideals.

One day, while Aurelius was in this state of great despair and frustration, an extraordinary thing happened.

Desperately depressed, Aurelius went out to a garden and threw himself down under a tree. With tears flooding his face, he begged God to deliver him from his impurity. For a time he lay there crying, then he heard a strange sound. It seemed to come from the house next door. It sounded like the voice of a child. Over and over he heard what sounded like a child singing, "Take up and read; take up and read."

Aurelius took this occurrence as a mysterious sign from God. Immediately his face brightened, and he ran to look for his book of the writings of Paul. When he found the book, he opened it and began reading. His eyes fell on these words: "Not in orgies and drunkenness, not in sexual immorality and debauchery, not in dissension and jealousy. Rather, clothe yourselves with the Lord Jesus Christ, and do not think about how to gratify the desires of the sinful nature" (Romans 13:13–14).

"Take up and read." These four mysterious words—backed by a mother's prayer and a searching heart—led to a sovereign encounter with Scripture. Later, in his famous work *Confessions*, Aurelius Augustine (also known as Saint Augustine) described his conversion experience: "I had no wish to read further and no need. For in that instant, with the very ending of the sentence, it was as though a light of utter confidence shone in all my heart, and all the darkness of uncertainty vanished away."

Augustine showed the passage to a friend who was nearby, and after reading the same page of Scripture, he, too, gave his life to Christ. Then together they rushed to tell the one person in the world who most wanted to hear of it. Describing the scene,

Augustine wrote, "Then we went in to my mother and told her, to her great joy. We related how it had come about: she was filled with triumphant exultation, and praised You who are mighty beyond what we ask or conceive: for she saw that You had given her more than with all her pitiful weeping she had ever asked."[2]

Saint Augustine, later appointed Bishop of Hippo (northern Africa), is known today as perhaps the greatest Christian philosopher and theologian of all time.

YOU MIGHT LIKE TO KNOW

Augustine was baptized by his mentor, Ambrose, the bishop of Milan, on Easter 387. His illegitimate son, Adeodatus, and the friend who was converted with him were also baptized. Among his many works, Augustine composed numerous commentaries on Psalms, the Sermon on the Mount, and the letters of Paul. Two years after becoming a bishop, at the age of forty-three, he began work on *Confessions*, which is still considered a masterpiece among the world's devotional literature.[3] The influence of his life and works on Western Christian leaders and culture is incalculable. Having seen her prayers answered, Augustine's mother died not long after he became a Christian.

∞

Handing the Sword to a Samurai

True heroism is remarkably sober, very undramatic. It is not the urge to surpass all others at whatever cost, but the urge to serve others at whatever cost.

—ARTHUR ASHE

Shortly after World War II, an eighteen-year-old girl named Peggy volunteered to help at a Japanese prisoner-of-war camp. The prisoners despised Americans, but Peggy's smiling sweetness soon made their confinement more palatable. "If you're uncomfortable or need anything, let me know," she often said. "I'll do anything I can to help."

Peggy was a tireless worker whose servant heart made an impression on the soldiers. But they didn't understand her kindness. They were the enemy. Why was she treating them like friends?

A few of the prisoners spoke English, so one day one of them asked her, "Why are you being so kind to us?"

Her answer was inconceivable. "Because Japanese soldiers killed my parents."

The prisoners stared in disbelief as Peggy recounted the events that led to her parents' death. Before the war, they had been missionary teachers in Yokohama, Japan, but when things got dangerous, they moved to Manilla. Then the Japanese captured Manilla, so Peggy's parents fled to the hills. But when the Americans won Manilla back, Japanese soldiers ran into the hills and captured the missionaries. Peggy's parents had a radio that the soldiers believed to be a secret communications piece. And after charging them as spies, the Japanese beheaded them.

Peggy was at school in America at the time and didn't find out about her parents' murder until after the war. At first she hated the Japanese. But the more she prayed and thought about the lives and ministry of her parents, the more she became convinced that forgiveness was what they would have wanted her to display. So following Christ's command, Peggy forgave the Japanese and devoted her time to helping the prisoners.

When these soldiers returned to Japan, one of them related Peggy's story to Mitsuo Fuchida, a high-ranking Japanese military officer. Mitsuo had assigned himself to investigate American prisoner-of-war camps. He was searching for examples of inhumane treatment, but Peggy's story was the exact opposite of what he had hoped to find.

When he heard the girl's story, Fuchida was overwhelmed and fascinated by it. How could a grieving teenager be so kind? The experience was foreign to Fuchida. In his country, it was the duty of a family member to take revenge for the death of a relative. Forgiveness was inconceivable. He couldn't shake the thought of this orphaned Christian girl serving the Japanese men.

Fuchida questioned all the prisoners who had known Peggy to confirm the story. Then he went so far as to contact his Filipino sources to learn what had happened to her parents. He discovered that as the husband and wife prepared to die, they had united in prayer.

Not long after this, Fuchida noticed an American soldier passing out tracts in a public square. As Fuchida walked by, the soldier handed him a tract titled *I Was a Prisoner of Japan*. Since prisoners concerned Fuchida, he immediately stopped and read the flier.

Later that day, Fuchida saw an advertisement for a book by the same American sergeant. It was available in Japanese, so Fuchida bought a copy. The story recounted that after a bombing raid over Japan, the sergeant had been forced to ditch his airplane in occupied China. The Japanese captured the sergeant and a few other men. Three officers were executed while the rest were sentenced to life imprisonment. The sergeant was beaten, nearly starved to death, and was consumed with hatred for the Japanese. Then after two years of imprisonment, the sergeant asked for the Bible that was secretly circulating through the camp. He had to wait his turn, but when he got it, he was allowed to keep it for three weeks. Racing through the Bible, the sergeant memorized large passages, and by the end of his three weeks, he had committed his life to Christ. His was such a true conversion that the sergeant promised God he would return to Japan as a missionary if he ever got out of prison. And when the war finally ended and the man was released, he became a missionary and set sail for Japan just as he promised.

Here was yet another amazing account of Christian love and forgiveness erasing hate. And this story had an even greater impact on Fuchida because he understood the mind-set of a military man.

The sergeant's tract and the girl's forgiving words made the difference for Fuchida. Now he wanted to read the Bible in order to understand what drove these people called Christians. As he headed for the bookstore, he passed the same spot where the American had been handing out tracts. This time a Japanese man in a business suit was there, shouting, "Get your Bible—food for your soul!" The coincidence startled Fuchida, and he bought a copy. But the Bible was not easy reading, and he put it away for nine months.

Then one morning, a Japanese newspaper columnist challenged his readers to read any thirty pages in the Bible, promising that they would find something there to touch their hearts. Fuchida took the challenge and started reading his Bible every day. After a time, he came upon the account of Christ's crucifixion. There it was again in Luke 23:34: "Father, forgive them, for they do not know what they are doing." Tears filled Fuchida's eyes. What forgiveness from the heart of a dying Savior!

By the time he finished the Book of Luke, Mitsuo Fuchida, the Samurai pilot who had led the air attack on Pearl Harbor, had given his heart to Jesus Christ.

YOU MIGHT LIKE TO KNOW

Fuchida was present at the formal Japanese surrender to the allies on board the U.S.S. *Missouri*. After his conversion and initial testimony in Japan, Mitsuo Fuchida was a frequent speaker in the United States. He was a friend of Billy Graham, and for thirty years he ministered as a full-time evangelist, telling his story all over the world. On the twenty-fifth anniversary of the attack on Pearl Harbor, Fuchida returned to Hawaii and stood under a tree as more than five thousand Americans honored the soldiers who died there. The ceremony began at the precise time of Fuchida's attack. At one point, Fuchida wandered off and knelt at the white grave marker of a Detroit, Michigan ensign. Then he visited the U.S.S. *Arizona*, where he sat for a time and prayed. His children became United States citizens. Mitsuo Fuchida died in his homeland.[4]

∞

The General and the Agnostic

Your influence is negative or positive, never neutral.
—HENRIETTA MEARS

One day in 1876, Lew Wallace boarded a train for Indianapolis. At the time, as far as he knew, he was simply on his way to a convention. But looking back, he would one day see that this routine trip led him to two of the most significant events in his illustrious life.

As a boy, Lew was often truant from school, preferring instead to be reading, fishing, or drawing. He was a dreamer, and his father had fits over all the money he had wasted on his education. For a time, art was Lew's first love; but after being beaten for drawing a caricature of his teacher, Lew turned his attention to writing.

One day a tutor handed Lew a copy of the New Testament and told him to read the story of the birth of Christ. He had attended church as a boy, but reading the Bible was new to him. During this assignment came his first encounter with the story of the wise men. The teacher also encouraged him to write poems, essays, and even his first novel.

But Lew continued to piddle with the rest of his education, so his father cut off all financial support. With no option but to work, Lew got a job copying documents. And for cheap entertainment, he read books in the statehouse library. It was about this time that he began scratching notes for a novel called *The Fair God*, a book that would take him the next thirty years to finish.

Lew went on to study law, but he also longed for the glory of war. When he learned that a war was brewing with Mexico, he gathered a troop and set out for Texas. But his efforts and excitement were wasted. He never fought in a battle, and on the way home, the last of his money was stolen.

Then the Civil War broke out, and Lew was called on to help. He quickly rose in rank and, by March 1862, became the youngest man to be appointed major general. But the battle of Shiloh was a disgrace for him when he marched sixty-five hundred men in the wrong direction. This fiasco cooled his reputation for the rest of the war. But a chance came to redeem himself when he saved Washington, D.C., from a sneak attack of the enemy that, had it succeeded, might have changed the course of American history.

When the war finally ended, Lew practiced law and finished his book, *A Fair God*, declared by many as one of the best novels of its time.

In 1878, Lew was offered the governorship of the New Mexico Territory. There he met Billy the Kid. At a face-to-face meeting with the outlaw, Lew agreed to pardon him on the condition that he turn in a large number of other criminals. The twenty-one-year-old Kid initially agreed but then reneged, committed more murders, threatened to kill the governor, and was eventually gunned down.

After three years in the Wild West, Lew was ready for a more peaceful existence. He returned to his home in Indiana and began thinking about his next writing project.

One day, an idea about the wise men from the story of Christ resurfaced. Lew was not a religious man, but the wise men seemed like a mysterious and interesting enough subject to use as the basis for a novel. So he wrote the story, carrying it through to the birth of Christ. But when the first draft was completed, he stuck the manuscript in a drawer and forgot about it.

Then Lew took his memorable train ride. While traveling to a National Soldiers Reunion, he struck up a conversation with long-time friend Colonel Robert Ingersoll, an open opponent of God.

After a few moments of chitchat, Lew decided to talk with Ingersoll about his religious beliefs. He asked Ingersoll if he believed in God, the devil, heaven, or hell. Ingersoll answered, "I don't know; do you?" Then according to Lew, Ingersoll's answer began "flowing like a heated river…the like of which I had never heard. He surpassed himself, and that is saying a great deal."[5]

Ingersoll's oratorical reply took the next two hours to deliver and was responsible for launching the general into the most significant phase of his already illustrious life.

Stepping down from the train, Lew was disturbed and provoked. Colonel Ingersoll's arguments did not cause him to doubt
God; instead, they fueled his need for rebuttal. Of the encounter,
Lew later said, "I was aroused for the first time in my life to the
importance of religion...[and] I resolved to study the subject.
While casting round how to set about the study to the best advantage, I thought of the manuscript in my desk. Its closing scene was
the child Christ in the cave by Bethlehem: why not go on with the
story down to the crucifixion?"[6]

Lew decided to "make over his unfinished novel into a reply to
Ingersoll."[7]

On the trail of a new conquest, Lew went to work on the book
of his life. He visited the Library of Congress and learned all he
could about the Jews. He studied the works of Edward Gibbon and
Josephus. Then he bought books and maps and had them shipped
to Indiana. At home, Lew tacked up a large map, organized his
materials, and began his research. The book took him seven years,
but in 1880, the epic *Ben-Hur*, one of the best-selling novels of all
time, was finally published.

Of his phenomenal book and the eventful train-ride discussion
that changed his life, the author wrote, "It only remains to say that
I did as I resolved, with results—first, the book *Ben-Hur*, and second, a conviction amounting to absolute belief in God and the
divinity of Christ."[8]

YOU MIGHT LIKE TO KNOW

The novel *Ben-Hur* depicts the conflict between a Roman cen-
turion and Judah Ben-Hur, a wealthy Hebrew who eventually
comes to Christ. A bootleg movie version of *Ben-Hur* was made in
1907. A lawsuit by Lew Wallace's son and publisher was fought and

won in the Supreme Court, making it the first successful copyright battle in motion-picture history. [9]

The Broadway play ran for twenty-one years and was seen by more than twenty million people. The 1959 film required fifty thousand extras. It won eleven Academy Awards, including Best Picture and Best Actor (Charlton Heston).[10]

After *Ben-Hur* was published, President Garfield, a friend and literary fan, offered Wallace his choice of the consulates of Brazil, Holland, Bolivia, and the Ottoman Empire (Turkey). Wallace chose the Ottoman Empire, which at that time spanned three continents. While serving in that region, he became the first "infidel" in six hundred years to shake the hand of a sultan.[11]

∞

A Volatile Visitation

Some men have thousands of reasons why they cannot do what they want to, when all they need is one reason why they can.

—WILLIS WHITNEY

Larry believed in God, but he certainly had no time for religion. He was a busy department head for General Electric at the Kennedy Space Center, where most of the guys he knew were atheists. His comfort zone was a productive, scientific environment, so he wasn't particularly happy when his wife began bringing her new Christian friends around the house.

Larry and Judy had met in high school and married young. Larry enlisted in the air force and then entered college. But to pay for his education, he had to get a job at Cape Canaveral that required him to get up at 3:00 A.M., work till 3:00 P.M., then race off to night school an hour and a half away. He followed this grueling routine for seven years. Judy rarely saw her husband, and for most of those years, she raised their four children alone.

Larry's drive and work ethic were forged early in life. He came from a family of nine children. His father was often out of work for years at a time, and his mother lived in perpetual exhaustion and discouragement. Poverty continually threatened them, so Larry determined he would make as much money as he could and never be poor again.

When he was nine years old, Larry started working on weekends. At fourteen, he was earning money as a singer at a movie theater that featured live entertainment between shows. He was never without a way to make money. His determination to get ahead consumed him and eventually affected his relationship with Judy.

While Larry was working for General Electric, Judy began attending services at the Park Avenue Baptist Church in Titusville, Florida. There she was introduced to Christ and became a Christian. For the next three years, she took the kids to church and made her best effort to live a committed Christian life in front of her husband. But Larry wasn't interested. Religion was fine for Judy, but Larry's plate was already full without adding God.

Every once in a while, folks from the church would come to the house and witness to Larry. For a time he was tolerant and polite, but after a while he became irritated with their sharing. Then an incident occurred that really rattled him.

One night Judy's pastor dropped by. This made the sixth time he had been out to visit Larry. Larry gave his usual polite responses, and then the conversation turned hostile. Irritated and fed up with what felt to him like badgering, Larry began to interrupt the pastor and argue every point the man tried to make. Then the pastor, frustrated by Larry's stubbornness, argued back. "Finally," Larry recalls later, the pastor "got so angry he got up and stormed out of the house, slamming the door as he left. Then about twenty seconds later he stuck his head back in and said, 'You know what [Larry], you're going to hell!' Then he slammed the door again and left."[12]

This was a pretty direct hit. But it must have done the trick, because not long after this, Larry went to church with his family and committed his life to Christ.

About two years later, Larry met Bill Bright of Campus Crusade for Christ. Bright had been talking with one of Larry's friends about starting a financial ministry. Larry's friend recommended him for the job, and six months later, Larry went to work for Campus Crusade, traveling around the country helping staff members get a better handle on their budgets.

Then Larry began to study biblical financial principles and share his findings with businessmen in his church, writing books and materials on the subject. Before long, Larry Burkett, the once-uninterested agnostic, left Campus Crusade to become the founder of Christian Financial Concepts, the foremost Christian financial training and counseling organization in the world.

YOU MIGHT LIKE TO KNOW

Larry Burkett first went on the radio in 1982 as a guest on the *Focus on the Family* radio broadcast with Dr. James Dobson. In 1999, the National Religious Broadcasters named Larry's radio program, *Money Matters,* Talk Show of the Year. The program airs on 388 stations.

Larry has more than seventy books and manuals in print.[13] His book *Damaged but Not Broken* describes his recent bout with cancer. Since Larry's earlier failure to spend time with his kids, he has made a commitment to never work more than fifty hours a week. Larry has been counseling people with their finances for more than thirty years.[14]

CONVERSION AND THE WORD OF GOD

As the rain and the snow come down from heaven, and do not return to it without watering the earth and making it bud and flourish…so is my word that goes out from my mouth: It will not return to me empty, but will accomplish what I desire and achieve the purpose for which I sent it.

—ISAIAH 55:10–11

How often have we kept silent when we could have spoken for Christ? How many times have we let a great opportunity slide, not out of fear or lack of love, but out of our own lack of faith that anything will result from it? Maybe we've had a bad experience. Or maybe, after years of sharing and praying for a relative, we've become discouraged because we've failed to see even the slightest change in that person's spiritual interest.

When this happens, we must shift the weight of our worry, placing the burden of success on God's Word, not on our expertise or our neighbor's receptivity. Yes, we are the messengers, but the Word has a life of its own. And yes, we are the truth takers, but the Truth can also take care of itself. How freeing for us when we recognize that the unassisted Word of God is teeming with life.

Yes, we scope the land in search of a patch in which to drop our seed. And yes, we may carry the water jug. But for all the fuss about our part, once the seed has landed, God is already at work. The good news is that after we have done our job, all heaven is brought to bear on the result. And if we'll trust God's process and pray, a harvest is promised to come.

BOOST YOUR OWN WORD POWER

Who do you know, right now, that is in need of a word from God? Ninety-nine percent of the people you know or will soon meet are dying for hope. Take it to them! Make a list of Scripture promises. Keep them handy at work or in the car. Do be sensitive, but don't be shy. Share as the Spirit leads. Write a note, include a scripture verse, then leave it on someone's windshield. Find a gospel tract that fits your style of evangelism. Learn it well, then pray for divine appointments to share it. When someone discusses a problem with you, if possible, pray for him or her at that moment or write a note or make a call saying that you've prayed for them. Keep your eyes peeled and your ears open. Purpose this month to actively seek opportunities to make payments on someone else's eternal security.

A word aptly spoken is like apples of gold
in settings of silver.

—PROVERBS 25:11

7

CHOICE WORDS OF CLARITY

For the Love of the Game

In the time we have it is surely our duty to do all the good we can to all the people we can in all the ways we can.

—WILLIAM BARCLAY

It was the year the Dodgers beat the Twins in the World Series. Baseball fever was winding down in Spartanburg, South Carolina, and sitting in the front office of the Philadelphia Phillies farm club was a young general manager named Pat.

This was Pat's first experience behind a desk. He had always been a ballplayer, but this year he had hung up his cleats and moved inside to a desk job. As a rookie manager, he knew there would be a learning curve, but he hadn't expected a losing season his first time at bat.

Pat had poured seven months of sixteen-hour days into his team, and at the end of the season, he had nothing to show for it.

He was a fierce competitor, so his team's losing record made him feel like a failure.

Trying to make some sense of it all, Pat picked up the phone and called his friend Bill Veeck. Bill was a mentor of sorts who had many years of experience in management. No doubt he had been down this road plenty of times himself. Bill would know what to do.

As Pat dumped out his frustration, Bill just patiently listened. When Pat was through, Bill asked, "Pat, just how many people did you draw to the ballpark this season?"

"One hundred and fourteen thousand."

"How many of those people were entertained and had a good time?"

"I guess all of them."

"Well," said Bill, "tell me one other thing you could have done this summer that would have provided as much fun, enjoyment, and entertainment to that many people?"

Pat couldn't think of anything.

Bill's next statement turned out to be some of the best advice a man in Pat's position would ever hear: "Listen, Pat, you never, ever have to apologize for showing people a fun time."[1]

What a great thought! You never have to apologize for showing people a good time. Pat had focused so hard on the fight that he'd forgotten about the fun. From that moment, he purposed to keep a more balanced tension between his drive to win and the entertainment value he was providing for the fans.

Bill's speech must have worked, because it has been nearly thirty-five years now, and Pat Williams, senior executive vice president of the Orlando Magic, is known throughout the country as one of pro sports' most zany and flamboyant promoters.[2]

A few years after Pat's call to Bill, Pat moved his entertainment expertise into the arenas of the National Basketball Association. He worked with the Chicago Bulls, Atlanta Hawks, and the Philadelphia Tigers. In 1987, Pat Williams became the cofounder of the Orlando Magic. He has led twenty of his teams to thrill millions of fans by going to the NBA playoffs, and five of those teams have made it to the NBA finals. In 1996, a national magazine named Pat Williams as one of the fifty most influential people in NBA history. He has motivated thousands of people with nineteen books, including his most recent, *Mr. Little John's Secrets to a Lifetime of Success.* Pat is considered one of America's premier motivational speakers, having addressed most of the Fortune 500 companies. He has also been a featured speaker at two Billy Graham crusades.[3]

Today, thanks to his relentless perseverance, the grace of God, and a little help from his friend Bill Veeck, Pat Williams is a perennial winner at showing the world a great time!

YOU MIGHT LIKE TO KNOW

Pat Williams and his wife, Ruth, are the parents of nineteen children, fourteen of whom were adopted. Pat teaches Sunday school at the First Baptist Church of Orlando, has run fourteen marathons, and has climbed Mount Rainer. He played college baseball for Wake Forest University and is in their Hall of Fame. Pat is known in the sports world as a consummate promoter and astute talent scout. He played a key role in bringing the WNBA to Orlando, and he won back-to-back first-round draft picks for the Magic in the 1992 and 1993 NBA lotteries.

∞

"Don't Send Any More Checks"

*Help people have great thoughts about themselves,
and they will begin to live like the people they can become.*

—JOHN MAXWELL AND JIM DORMAN

Stella knew better, but she didn't care. She was going to make money any way she could, even if it was illegal—even if she had to steal it from the government.

Every month when her medical stickers came from the welfare department, Stella sold them to the highest bidder and pocketed the cash. Some of her "clients" used the stickers to get their teeth fixed; others used them for abortions.

Stella wasn't raised to live like this. Her father was a noncommissioned officer in the air force, and her mother was a beautician. But after high school, Stella and a girlfriend wanted to "live glamorous lives and dance on the black television show *Soul Train*," so they took the three hundred dollars they had saved and moved to Hollywood.

In California, Stella was wild and promiscuous. Within three years, she had four abortions and then became pregnant for the fifth time. But by now, Stella was feeling the weight of her wasted life. She decided to carry her baby, but to do this she would have to go on welfare. So she quit her job in circulation at the *Los Angeles Times* and began three and a half years of scamming the government. With a $465-per-month welfare check, food stamps, and an "under the table" part-time job, Stella could make more money than most folks working forty-hour weeks.

One day, Stella walked into an advertising agency looking for more under-the-table work. But instead of finding a job, she found Jesus. The three men running the small company shared Christ with her and told her that they only hired Christians. The men pulled out a Bible and led Stella through a prayer of salvation. Though she meant what she prayed, Stella wasn't ready to change her lifestyle.

Then a month before her baby was due, she developed a medical condition that forced her to have an emergency Cesarean section. She was in the hospital for a week and a half, and her only visitor was one of the men from the agency.

After the baby came, Stella went right back to partying. Most days she just dropped the child off at a government day-care center, sold a few medical stickers to buy drugs, and hung out at Venice Beach.

But the man at the ad agency kept calling to check on her and to invite her to church. After nearly a year, Stella finally agreed to go.

Stella immediately loved the Crenshaw Christian Center. At the end of the service, she walked down front and gave her life to the Lord.

In the weeks that followed, people at the church took interest in her, invited her to their homes, and encouraged her faith. For the first time, Stella saw true Christian families—husbands and wives who were committed to staying married—and she began to want the same thing. One couple talked to her about going back to school, which led to her living with other single mothers to save money and swap baby-sitting.

Stella eventually stopped doing drugs and sleeping around. But quitting welfare was something else entirely. She had become dependent on it and couldn't see any way to manage without it.

Then one Sunday, Stella was sitting in the back of the church when she heard the words that would alter her life beyond recognition. The pastor was preaching, and all at once, in a passionate pitch, he shouted out, "What are you doing living on welfare? The government is not your source; God is!"[4]

Stella knew this was a word from God just for her. She sat there stunned. Then she thought that if God could make the universe, he could certainly take care of her and her baby.

The next morning, a nervous Stella wrote a letter to her caseworker, saying, "Don't send any more checks." And within three months, she was hired at a food-distribution company for good pay.

Then in 1984, with the help of a host of friends, she launched her own magazine for Christian singles. In the first year, she distributed one hundred thousand magazines and put fifty thousand dollars in the bank.

All seemed to be going well until riots broke out in Los Angeles in 1992. The violence shut down the businesses of Stella's advertisers, which eventually hit her income and caused her magazine to fold.

Stella was incensed. "I couldn't swallow that," she said later. "Some thugs broke the law, looted these businesses, and destroyed an entire business district. I spoke out, calling these folks the criminals that they were."[5]

Stella's outspoken comments got national attention. She was asked to do her own call-in radio show in Los Angeles. Local stations began to carry her views, and she founded the Coalition on Urban Renewal and Education.

Stella, the girl who had once been on drugs and welfare, now regularly found herself on national television. She spoke on C-Span, then other speaking engagements followed. Stella (which means "star" in Italian) changed her first name to Star, and before long, Star Parker was making appearances on programs like *Oprah* and *Larry King Live.*

Eight years later, the outspoken Star Parker is now a mother of two, author, political activist, and motivational speaker who speaks out against the welfare system and "blind" black loyalty to the Democratic Party. Because of her own success as a young, black female entrepreneur, she espouses the virtues of the free-market enterprise system, believing it and the church are the best solutions for fighting crime, poverty, and unemployment. Star welcomes the opportunities she is regularly given to pit her conservative views against powerful black leaders such as Jesse Jackson. And concerning the church she says, "The church is the one with the best track record of getting people out of poverty, off drugs, out of lawlessness and sexual promiscuity, into employment, and into lifelong marriages."[6]

YOU MIGHT LIKE TO KNOW

Star lives in Southern California with her two daughters, Angel and Rachel. She has addressed the Republican National Convention, has been a guest on Rush Limbaugh's radio program, and is a friend of Alan Keyes. On welfare reform and the dramatic turnaround in her life, she has said, "I am not pushing one solution or one cure-all program. What I am saying is I am a traditionalist. I believe in family and faith. And I am a testament to what anyone can do if they take that first step."[7]

∞

Taylor-Made Devotions

Should our names perish, may the truths we taught, the virtues we cultivated, the good works we initiated live on and blossom with undying energy.

—CHARLES SPURGEON

Ken had his hands full. Every night when he walked in the door from work, a great throng of children descended upon him. It seemed that every time he turned around, a new one was showing up. By the time the last child was born, he was just one player short of a football squad. Life was never dull at Ken's house—except when it came time for Bible reading.

Every night after dinner, Ken read the Bible to his children. It was something his dad did with him and his brothers growing up. Even now, he could still remember his father say, "Unless you fellows get into the Word of God and get the Word of God into your lives, you'll never amount to anything."

So just like when he was a boy, Ken gathered his family around him and read aloud from the King James Bible. The King James Bible was the version almost every Protestant used in the early fifties, even though the language was more than three centuries old. People knew the Bible was good for them, even if it was tough to translate, so like castor oil they guzzled their daily dose and, with reverence, endured it the best they could.

But like many others, Ken had personally struggled with the discrepancy between the language he spoke and the Scriptures he read. And the problem with these differences was never more magnified than when he led family devotions.

His children were young, and it was hard enough keeping them still without adding the strain of helping them decipher the passages. But night after night, Ken valiantly gave it a try. To pique their interest, he read a section in the King James first and then asked the children questions afterward. And when he came upon an unusual word, he would stop and try to make sense of it.

One night, Ken had just finished reading one of those difficult verses when one of his little girls looked up and asked, "Well, if that's what it means, why doesn't it say so?"

Ken agreed. If the Word of God is living and active, sharper than any double-edged sword, then he certainly didn't want his children feeling it was dead and dull. He decided that if his children were going to understand the Bible, he was going to have to give it to them in an understandable form. So before the next devotional time, he wrote out a verse then paraphrased it in his own words. And that night when he introduced his own paraphrased version of the Bible, his kids were much more responsive.

Ken knew he was on to something.

After this experience, every day as he rode to work on the train, Ken took part of a chapter from the Epistles and wrote it out in his own words. Then in the evening, after the kids were in bed, he checked his own ideas against original Greek word studies. Finally one afternoon in late December 1960, Kenneth Taylor finished the final version of his paraphrase of the New Testament. It had taken him seven years to complete.

Thinking his work might appeal beyond the scope of his family, Ken decided to publish his paraphrase. Since he worked at a publishing firm, he thought it would be easy. But when he took his manuscript around to a few publishers, none of them were interested. Most of them said they didn't see a demand for another version of the Bible.

Discouraged but still determined, Ken and his wife, Margaret, decided to print the book on their own. And with a small bit of savings and a printer friend's help, the first two thousand copies of *Living Letters* were printed.

Then Ken took his book to the 1962 Christian Booksellers' Convention and sold nearly nine hundred copies. Within a year, seventy-five thousand more were sold. And then one day, Billy Graham was handed a copy in the hospital. He liked it so much that he ordered fifty thousand copies to distribute to viewers of his television program. Eventually the Billy Graham Association distributed six hundred thousand copies of *Living Letters*.

By 1971, Ken Taylor had finished paraphrasing both the Old and the New Testament and called his work *The Living Bible*, which today shows sales of more than forty million copies.

The reception of *The Living Bible* was unprecedented. Ken stood to make a great deal of money but had already decided not to take a dime of profit. Because it was God's Word, Ken wanted all the proceeds invested back into the kingdom. He did this by setting up the Tyndale House Foundation to receive all royalties.

Not long after Ken began work on *The Living Bible*, he left his position at Moody Press to form a new publishing company. He named it Tyndale House, after the courageous fourteenth-century Bible translator, William Tyndale. Tyndale was the first to attempt publication of an English version of the Bible, and he was burned at the stake in 1535 because of it.

What started nearly fifty years ago as one father's wish to make the Bible "say what it means" has now emerged as one of the largest and most respected Christian publishing houses in the world.

YOU MIGHT LIKE TO KNOW

Ken Taylor gave his life to Christ as a young child but was significantly influenced toward an even more wholehearted commitment after reading a book on the life of athlete, millionaire, and missionary William Borden.

In an effort to update *The Living Bible*, Ken Taylor and Tyndale gathered a team of ninety biblical scholars who, over a period of eight years, produced *The New Living Translation*, which was introduced in 1996. The Tyndale House Publishing Company reaches every continent in the world. Ken Taylor's *The Bible in Pictures for Little Eyes*, a children's devotional Bible, has sold more than one million copies in more than sixty languages. Ken Taylor is also the author of *My Life: a Guided Tour: The Autobiography of Kenneth N. Taylor*. A handwritten note on a wall in the Taylor home says: "Finished final revision of paraphrase *Living Letters* at 3:00 P.M. today with praise to the Lord. December 27, 1960."[8]

∞

She Wouldn't Take No for an Answer

The greatest thing any person can do for another is to confirm
the deepest thing in him, in her—to take the time and have the
discernment to see what is most deeply there, most fully that person,
and then confirm it by recognizing and encouraging it.

—MARTIN BUBER

In 1980, a group of Riverside, California, homemakers decided to meet each week for a neighborhood Bible study. The organizer of the group was a perky, middle-aged mother of two named Emilie, and the speaker was a vivacious, gifted Bible teacher named Florence.

The Bible study was instantly popular. Each week the numbers grew, until the home they were meeting in could no longer hold all the enthusiastic women.

One evening when Emilie and Florence were out to dinner with their husbands, one of the men suggested that they change the format of their meeting from a Bible study to a seminar in order to accommodate the rapid growth of their group. The two agreed to try it, and with Florence teaching and Emilie sharing household management tips, the first "Feminar" was born.

Then one day, at the height of the Feminar's success, Florence, who had already authored two books of her own, looked at Emilie and popped an outrageous question: "Why don't you write a book? All this information you're sharing is invaluable. Let's put it in a book so even more women can benefit from it."

"Florence, I haven't even the slightest desire to write a book," Emilie said.

"Well, I think you should do it," Florence argued.

"Well, I'm not going to."

"Oh, yes you will!"

"Oh, no I won't! Look, we both know I just have a high-school diploma. I wouldn't know the first thing about writing a book. Besides, I don't even like to write!"

But Florence was adamant. "Emilie, you're going to write a book."

A few weeks later, Emilie was at home when the telephone rang. It was Bob Hawkins Sr., the president of Harvest House Publishers. "Hello, Emilie!" he said. "I understand you have a book on home organization that we might be interested in."

For a moment Emilie was speechless. When she recovered, she

said, "No. I think there's been a mistake. You see, I'm not a writer. I wouldn't even know how to go about writing a book."

"Well," the publisher went on, "do you have any tapes of your talks?"

"I have a few tapes, maybe eight or so—but how does that help you?"

"I'll tell you what. Why don't you just pack the tapes up and send them to us. We'll take it from there."

So Emilie sent her eight cassette tapes off to the publisher, and some months later, without touching a typewriter, the Riverside, California, mother of two found herself clutching a book with her name on it, titled *More Hours in My Day*.

It's been more than twenty years since world-class author and motivational speaker Florence Littauer spoke the words "You need to write a book," but that's exactly what God used to launch the internationally recognized writing and speaking ministry of her close friend Emilie Barnes.

Of her inaugural publishing experience, Emilie said, "Everything I knew was in that first little book. I really thought that would be it. I had nothing else to say on the subject. But the Lord and my friend Florence had other ideas. They truly believed in me, a little high-school educated homemaker. They saw something in me that I didn't even see in myself. And one by one more books came."[9]

Thanks to the persistent words of Florence Littauer, as well as the loving partnership of her husband, Bob, Emilie has been privileged to touch the lives of hundreds of thousands of women in person and on video. The woman who said she couldn't write has now authored more than fifty books, including *Welcome Home, Beautiful Home on a Budget,* and *If Teacups Could Talk*.

YOU MIGHT LIKE TO KNOW

Emilie Barnes was raised in a Jewish family and converted to Christianity as a teenager. At age seventeen, she married her high-school sweetheart, Bob, who has partnered with her in full-time ministry for more than twenty years.

∞

How Morse Cracked the Code

I would hurl words into the darkness and wait for an echo.
If an echo sounded, no matter how faintly,
I would send other words to tell, to march, to fight.

—RICHARD WRIGHT

Samuel Morse was born in Charleston, Massachusetts, to an illustrious and talented family. His mother was the daughter of Dr. Samuel Finely, one of the early presidents of Princeton University, and his father, the Reverend Jedidiah Morse, was a well-known preacher and evangelist, as well as the author of the first textbook on American geography.

At an early age, Samuel showed great artistic talent, and for many years it seemed that he might become famous for his paintings. When he was fourteen, he helped pay his way to Yale by painting the portraits of faculty members and students. After graduation, he studied art in London. He gained the reputation of being one of the best portrait painters in America, and in 1819, he was given the commission to paint the portrait of the Marquis de Lafayette at the White House.

But Samuel was interested in more than just canvas and oil paint. He was fascinated by electricity.

One day, in 1832, while sailing home from a trip to Europe, Morse struck up a conversation with a fellow passenger, Dr. Charles Jackson of Boston. Their discussion quickly moved to the subject of new scientific discoveries and electricity. Jackson happened to mention that "electricity passes instantly over any known length of wire. Benjamin Franklin passed current many miles and noticed no difference of time between the touch at one end and the spark at the other." This was a revolutionary thought to Morse, and it eventually became the catalyst for a wonderful new invention.

Morse reasoned that if Franklin's discovery were true, then it was highly probable that that same wire could transmit intelligence across any distance.

Back in the U.S., Samuel worked on constructing an electronic transmission device. To fund his experiments, he taught at New York University, continued to paint, and lived in a cheap, one-room apartment. Nine years later, the United States Congress passed an appropriation that enabled Samuel Morse to lay the first telegraph lines.

On the morning of May 24, 1844, two groups of people gathered for the sending of the first telegraph message. At one end of the line, at the nation's capital, stood Samuel, President James Madison's wife, and a group of other dignitaries. At the other end, in Baltimore, Maryland, Samuel's colleague Alfred Vail waited excitedly.

But what would be the first message? Morse decided not to choose the famous message but gave that honor to Annie Ellsworth, the daughter of the U.S. Commissioner of Patents.

Around 8:45 A.M., Morse began tapping out the very first electronic message. It was from the King James Bible and, amid cheering and celebration, was immediately and completely received in Baltimore. The message, from Numbers 23:23, was an interesting one. It said, "Surely there is no enchantment against Jacob, neither is there any divination against Israel: according to this time it shall be said of Jacob and of Israel, What hath God wrought!"[10]

YOU MIGHT LIKE TO KNOW

One hundred years later, Congress unveiled a bronze plaque commemorating Morse's achievement. At the top, it reads, "What Hath God Wrought!" The last portion states, "On May 24, 1944, the seventy-eighth Congress of the United States—Second Session—dedicated this memorial to the humility and vision which enabled this inventor to be the conveyor of this universal blessing to mankind."

GOD'S WORD OF CLARITY

*Jesus put his hands on the man's eyes. Then his eyes were opened,
his sight was restored, and he saw everything clearly.*
—MARK 8:25

Like it or not, our humanity presents us with certain limitations that only a heavenly hand can fix. We are born spiritually impaired, so it should never surprise us when we wake up and discover that we've been "blind" for quite some time.

We may have an annoying habit or a deeply embedded weakness that we are powerless to remove. Or sometimes, like sheep in God's pasture, we are victims of an enemy who has stealthily pulled the wool over our eyes.

Jesus knows we need help with our seeing. He is just waiting for us to know it too.

Maturity begins when we receive moments of challenge as welcome visitations from God, who has come to give us freedom, to take away our canes, and to call off the seeing-eye dogs.

Who among us would stay blind if given the chance to see? But so often we refuse the very hand that was sent to do surgery.

Christ is our constant lamp bearer, our inner illuminating source. And if we let him, he will sharpen our dullness, brighten our darkness, and magnify God's holiness in us. If we will risk handing in our old set of glasses, he will be faithful to fit us with a newer, stronger pair, ones more suitable for the next leg of our journey, a journey on which he has promised to walk beside us all the way.

BOOST YOUR OWN WORD POWER

Make an appointment with a friend, neighbor, or young person who has little adult encouragement. Notice the signs that you are being watched. No doubt there are people in your life who consider you their hero. They study your moves, imitate your dress, and hang on your every word. Make the most of your audience. Grant them a slice of your precious time. Provoke their potential. Promote their dreams. Applaud how far they've come, and listen to where they hope to go. Present pertinent scriptures. Share God's wisdom in Christlike love. Help them work through sticky issues, plan for college, or start a business. Offer practical insight from lessons someone taught you. Sign up for a discipling or mentoring program at your church or local high school. Invite someone you trust to give you suggestions that will make you a better person. Ask the Holy Spirit for your own "blind spot test." Do all the good you can in all the ways you can. Today leave a mark for eternity.

Say only what is good and helpful to those you are talking to, and what will give them a blessing.

—EPHESIANS 4:29 TLB

8

CHOICE WORDS OF CONCERN

Don't Pick Me, God

*Think of what would happen if just ten people
in any given church deliberately chose (to say to themselves)
"I know many people are burdened and hurting.
To whom can I speak with words of love and concern?"*

—LARRY CRABB

Every week, thousands of people turn to friends or acquaintances and say, "I'm going to church this Sunday. Would you like to come along?" Sometimes the answer is yes, and sometimes that yes leads to an amazing life transformation. One day that question was put to someone who was at the lowest point in her personal life, while at the highest point in her career.

Steve Slain was a strength-and-conditioning coach who had the reputation of being one of the best fitness trainers in central Florida. But he was different than most fitness trainers. He did not worship at the temple of his body; instead, he saw his body as the temple of God.

One day Steve was introduced to a new client named Michelle. Michelle was an athlete who was suffering from a disease called Chronic Fatigue and Immune Dysfunction Syndrome (CFIDS). But Michelle wasn't just any athlete—she was Michelle Akers, the world-champion women's soccer star.

At the time, Michelle looked like anything but a world champion. Her four-year marriage was ending, her body was racked with debilitating pain, and her spiritual life was practically nonexistent. Steve knew he could help her get back into shape, but he was going to have to pace his training according to Michelle's energy level. There was a lot of work to do. So Steve got right to work, putting first things first—he invited Michelle to church.

Michelle had gone to church before. In high school, she had even made a genuine commitment to Christ, but it was an understatement to say that a whole lot had happened to her since then.

After high school, Michelle attended the University of Central Florida on a soccer scholarship, where she was honored as a four-time All-American. She was such a phenomenal player there that upon graduation, the school retired her jersey. Then Michelle got married. In 1991, she was the leading scorer on the American team when they won the first ever Women's World Cup soccer final. In 1992, she played in Sweden and became the top scorer for both men and women in that country. Next she traveled the globe, promoting women's soccer and signing endorsements with Reebok, Umbro, and Proctor and Gamble. Finally, Michelle's health hit rock bottom—and her marriage was following right behind it. By the time Steve met Michelle, God had been missing from her picture for a long time.

But Michelle was open. There was something different about Steve. He was excited about Christ, got up every morning to pray and read his Bible, and talked constantly about his church, North-land Community. One day he asked Michelle to go with him, and she agreed.

After her first visit, Michelle went to church off and on. Then in the summer, she decided to take a trip to her family's cabin in the Cascade Mountains outside Seattle. She needed to get away so she could think, grieve her broken marriage, and get right with God.

At the cabin, Michelle listened to some worship and teaching tapes Steve had given her. The music made her feel peaceful, and the teaching nudged her closer to God. The more she listened, the more the tapes affected her. After a few weeks, Michelle was sure she was ready for a redirection in her life.

During this time, Michelle visited her grandparents in Seattle and went to church with them. As she listened to the preacher, she suddenly felt that God was trying to speak to her. She sensed he was asking her to make a total commitment, asking her to speak out and to call others to him.

Michelle was petrified. What would her fans think? She called her own shots. Who was she to speak for God? Could she handle the lifestyle change?

The sense of God's calling and her fear were so strong that Michelle called Steve from a pay phone on the way home. She didn't want to be known as a "spiritual nut." She certainly didn't want to miss out on any fun or be ridiculed.

Steve was able to calm Michelle's fears. When she returned to Orlando, she began to consistently attend church and Bible stud-ies. Gradually the changes came. And after months of praying, cry-ing, and studying, she was ready to give her all to God.

In 1995, the American team came in a disappointing third at the Women's World Cup. Michelle had been knocked unconscious within the first minutes of the game, and the whole team came home devastated. But this time, Michelle knew how to handle defeat and had someone greater to lean on.

Then in 1996, she found herself exhausted but elated, standing on top of the gold-medal podium at the Atlanta Olympics. Throughout the ceremony, she could only thank God. Later, in her journal she wrote—"August 2, 1996: My mind keeps returning to the past few years when I thought I was so alone, so isolated in my struggles and pain. God is so good. Through it all he was preparing me for this moment, this experience. So faithful. He took it all away, but he gave me back so much more. I go to bed tonight an Olympic Champion."

Then in her May 1996 address to the United States Congress concerning CFIDS, Michelle said, "Through the suffering and heartache, I have gained a strength and purpose that carries me when I cannot do it myself. I have seen and experienced God's grace and peace only because I have been in the valley. I now know it took this long visit in the depths of this illness to open myself to a more meaningful and purposeful life."[1]

YOU MIGHT LIKE TO KNOW

Michelle's Web site, www.michelleakers.com, and her book *The Game and the Glory* contain a clear explanation of God's plan of salvation. Michelle is the cofounder of Soccer Outreach International, a ministry she began "to maximize my international platform through…soccer, because it is the most popular game in the world.… We're just trying to use my story to rub elbows with a lot of athletes, media, officials.… We partner with different ministries…and train these agencies how to use soccer and sports as a ministry.... [Part of our mission is to] model how to use local ath-letes, resources, and events to evangelize."[2]

At one time, Michelle considered being the first female NFL player. She kicked a fifty-two-yard field goal in a tryout with the Dallas Cowboys. She was awarded Century Player of the Year 1999 (CONCACAF), ESPN Athlete of the Year 1985, U.S. Soccer Federation Female Player of the Year three times, and was a gold medalist at the 1998 Goodwill Games. She is a speaker for Campus Crusade for Christ, Fellowship of Christian Athletes, and the Billy Graham Association. She has been a board member for Sports Outreach America, U.S. Soccer Federation, Women's Sport Foundation, and founder of the Michelle Akers Fund (with CFIDS Association of America). Her motto is "Go hard or go home." Her biggest fear is "Not making my life and work count in God's eyes."[3]

$$\infty$$

Message on a Bottle

*A helping word to one in trouble is often like
a switch on a railroad track—there's only an inch
between a wreck and smooth rolling prosperity.*
—HENRY WARD BEECHER

Eighteen-year-old W. O. Lattimore had never been drunk, couldn't play a single card game, and had never been away from home. So when he enlisted in the army after the war broke out, he was in for a culture shock.

Lattimore's regiment was stocked with young guys who thought partying was their patriotic duty. The wildness of these men dazzled him, and before long, he could drink, gamble, and cuss like the best of them. But while his military status climbed to lieutenant, his morals plunged.

Older, seasoned officers pulled the young man aside to warn him about the consequences of his lifestyle, but Lattimore scoffed and remarked that his pursuits were harmless. He was soon addicted to alcohol, and his health and work suffered. Eventually, he was discharged from the army and tried to stop drinking, but every attempt failed. He even lost his family. Defeated and despondent, Lattimore destroyed all evidence of his identity and gave up on life.

Nearing death, Lattimore staggered into a church. A meeting was in progress, so he slouched on a bench until he realized the room was filled with happy, well-dressed people and wanted to leave. As he stood up, a man began to sing. The words and the music stirred Lattimore, and a strange sensation came over him. When the man sang the third verse, the words grabbed him.

> Sowing the seed of a lingering pain,
> Sowing the seed of a maddened brain,
> Sowing the seed of a tarnished name,
> Sowing the seed of eternal shame,
> Oh, what will the harvest be?"[4]

Lattimore bolted from the church and raced down a snow-piled street until he reached a bar. Hoping to drown out the music, he bought a bottle of whiskey. But it was too late—the words were stuck in his mind. On every bottle in the barroom Lattimore saw the phrase, "What will the harvest be?" The words were everywhere he looked. They seemed so real that he threw his glass, and it shattered on the floor.

The song hounded him for weeks, until one day he gave in and walked back to the church. As he came dragging in, a kind man opened his Bible and prayed with Lattimore to receive Jesus Christ. For the first time he heard that the Savior could cure his alcoholism. When he reached for the Lord that day, he was healed.

Sometime later, people wept as Mr. Lattimore stood before the church and shared his experience. A reporter happened to be there and was so moved by the story that he printed it in the newspaper. Then one day a letter came to the general post office addressed to Mr. Lattimore. It read:

Dear Papa:

Momma and I saw in the Chicago papers that a man had been saved in the meetings there, who was once a lieutenant in the army, and I told Momma that I thought it was my papa. Please write to us as soon as you can, as Momma cannot believe that it was you.

When the people of the church heard about the letter, they found a home for Mr. Lattimore and sent for his family. They helped him get a job and gave him numerous opportunities to tell his story. W. O. Lattimore became such a strong communicator that his friends encouraged him to study for the ministry. Eventually, the once-homeless derelict was called to be the pastor of a large church in Evanston, Illinois, where he served until his death in 1899.

On a snowy day in Chicago, W. O. Lattimore was yanked from the grave by the words of a song. He knew firsthand of the power of a few choice words set to music. He was so grateful for his redemption that he decided to write a song of his own, the famous hymn "Out of the Darkness into the Light."

YOU MIGHT LIKE TO KNOW

The song that W. O. Lattimore saw on the bottle, "What Shall the Harvest Be?" was penned by a bedridden woman who reported she had never been well a day in her life.

∞

Charlotte's Song

Believe, when you are most unhappy, that there is something for you to do in the world. So long as you can sweeten another's pain, life is not in vain.
—HELEN KELLER

Among the guests at dinner one evening at a home in the West End of London were a distinguished Swiss evangelist, Dr. Caesar Malan, and a frail, sickly woman named Charlotte.

At one point during the meal, the evangelist leaned over to Charlotte and asked about her spiritual condition. Charlotte was offended by this intrusion into an area she considered private and said that she would rather not discuss the subject. Dr. Malan quickly apologized, saying that he had not meant to offend her but that "he always liked to speak a word for his Master"[5] and that he hoped that one day she would dedicate her life to the work of the ministry.

About three weeks later, these two met again, but this time Charlotte was in a different frame of mind. After their previous dinner conversation, she had been plagued with thoughts of Christ and now wished desperately for Dr. Malan to tell her what she must do to come to him.

After counseling her for a few minutes, Dr. Malan concluded,

"You must come just as you are, a sinner, to the Lamb of God that taketh away the sin of the world."

Charlotte gave her life to Christ that day, and every year on that same date for the rest of her life, she celebrated the remembrance of it.

Charlotte's health continued to deteriorate until she was bedridden. One day, her brother, who was a pastor, decided to raise money to build a school for the children of poor clergymen. Charlotte offered to help with the task by writing a song. The song Charlotte wrote was called "Just As I Am."

Charlotte's hymn was an immediate success, and she was able to contribute more than half the money needed for the school from her royalty check. In 1836, she put the hymn in a collection of her original songs called *The Invalid's Hymn Book*. Of the hymn, her brother said, "In the course of a long ministry, I hope to have been permitted to see some fruit of my labors; but I feel more has been done by a single hymn of my sister's."

Charlotte Elliot lived to be eighty-two years old, though she was tormented with physical pain and suffering nearly all her life. Of her difficulties she once said, "God sees, God guards me. His grace surrounds me, and His voice continually bids me to be happy and holy in His service just where I am."

After the hymn "Amazing Grace," Charlotte's song, spawned from the words of the Swiss evangelist, has been sung by more people than any other hymn.

YOU MIGHT LIKE TO KNOW

Charlotte Elliott wrote approximately 150 hymns and was considered the greatest English woman hymn writer of all time. It was reported that after her death, more than one thousand letters were discovered from people who had given testimony to what "Just As I Am" had meant in their lives.[6] And for decades, "Just As I Am" has been the song sung around the world as millions walk forward to give their lives to Christ at Billy Graham crusades.

GOD'S WORD CONCERNING US

*Can a mother forget the baby at her breast and have no compassion
on the child she has borne? Though she may forget, I will not forget you!
See, I have engraved you on the palms of my hands.*

—ISAIAH 49:15–16

What makes it possible for us to show concern for others when
we have so many concerns of our own? How can we care for someone else when no one has shown interest in us? How often have we
heard of someone with health concerns, financial needs, or mari-
tal problems and we meant to call or stop by, but our own pressing
needs and complications prevented us from thinking beyond ourselves? Perhaps we are intimacy starved. Perhaps we are the dis-
connected offspring of a Father who, we believe, has run off and
left us.

It is difficult, if not impossible, to share cups of water from a
bone-dry well. Yet the paradox of faith is that sometimes the very
answer for our own impoverished souls is to offer what few droplets
we do have. Like the widow who was down to her last penny, we
will receive more when we spend what we have on someone who
has even less. But faith is required for such an action.

When we feel unloved, we have to ask ourselves where we got
off the boat with God. If we feel we're floundering at sea, most
likely it is we who have jumped ship or fallen overboard.

Maybe the closest we can come to perceiving God's care for us
is to think of a loving mother. Once her child is born, a mother is

on call twenty-four hours a day. Though she is frequently exhausted, she doesn't mind the effort. Her child is her sole delight. She is attentive to his tears. And though he does not understand her language, she talks to him, sings to him, and holds him lovingly. When her child grows up and moves away, a mother's eyes never tire of watching the road for his return. And when he is present, she is relentless—asking about his health, his companions, his nutrition, his safety, his progress, his comfort, his happiness, and a million other things she wants to know. For as long as he lives, a child is rooted in his mother's heart.

If this is true of an earthly mother, how much more devoted to us is our heavenly Father?

There is fuel to spare at our Father's house. We will be generous in our concern for others when we grasp how deeply we are loved, how decidedly we are wanted, and how desperately we are missed by our Father during those times we have wandered away.

BOOST YOUR OWN WORD POWER

Purpose to memorize scriptures that assure you of God's care for you. Repeat them to yourself several times a day. Sit quietly in God's presence and ask, "Lord, how do you feel about me today?" Write down the answer he gives—include everything that comes to your mind and heart. Receive correction but reject condemnation. Accept unconditionally God's unconditional love for you. Study the lives of great missionaries to learn what makes them tick. Where did they get their passion for Christ? How did they nurture their passion for people?

Determine never to leave church without praying for someone else's need. Make a point to find out the history of the "difficult" people in your life. Hearing their stories will help you better care for them. Offer to join a team from your church on crisis calls or hospital visits. Better yet, visit a hospital by yourself and talk to lonely patients who have no family or visitors. Call your mother.

She speaks with wisdom, and faithful instruction
is on her tongue.

—PROVERBS 31:26

9

CHOICE WORDS OF COMMERCE

How to Triple Your Income and Double Your Time Off

Each friend represents a world in us, a world possibly not born until they arrive, and it is only by this meeting that a new world is born.

—ANAIS NIN

The seminar was over, and as usual, Mark had wowed his audience. Folks filed by to shake his hand and thank him for his inspirational stories and for reminding them again that "free enterprise means that the more enterprising you are the freer you are."[1] Mark's talk that day was titled "How to Triple Your Income and Double Your Time Off." He didn't know it at the time, but he was moments away from meeting the man that was destined to help him triple his own income and double his own time off...many, many times over.

In the audience of Mark's seminar that day was a guy named Jack, who was also a motivational speaker. As Jack listened, something about Mark intrigued him. After the seminar, he introduced himself and asked Mark out to lunch.

As the two men got acquainted, something significant clicked between them. Soon they were making plans to windsurf off the California coast and setting regular breakfast appointments to talk over business ideas. Both men were idea machines. And they quickly discovered that the more ideas they bounced off each other, the better entrepreneurs and communicators they became.

Jack made a point of using great stories in his seminars. One day, at the end of one of his talks, a man asked, "You know that story about the dog that you told? Is that in a book somewhere?"[2] Jack had been asked this countless times, but this time he got the feeling that it was a divine question. The next time he got with Mark, he mentioned the incident. Mark confirmed that he, too, had had the same experience with people asking about his stories. And it was then that Jack Canfield and Mark Hansen knew that they were supposed to pool their best inspirational stories and write a book.

From the start, the men knew that the first, most important key of any book's success is the title. So they set about to find a title that would grab their readers by the heart. Each morning they woke up at 4:30 A.M. to think about the possibilities for a "mega-best-selling title." Then one morning in 1990, the phone rang at Mark's house in Newport Beach. It was Jack, and he had the title: *Chicken Soup for the Soul*.

Mark loved it! The title gave him goose bumps. Mark's wife, Patty, also loved the title, and so did Jack's wife, Georgia. However, the publishers they queried did not love it. "It's too nicey-nice," they said. And after thirty-three tries, their literary agent quit, leaving them on their own to find a publisher.

But Mark and Jack were determined. One of Mark's mottoes was "Every time you get rejected, say, 'Next!'"[3]

Next for Mark and Jack was a trip to the American Booksellers Convention. There they trudged from booth to booth, talking with any publisher who would listen until finally a company from Florida, Health Communications, agreed to print the first twenty thousand copies.

Instead of the three months the men expected, the process of publishing their book of 101 heartwarming stories took three years. But finally, in 1993, the first copy of *Chicken Soup for the Soul* was served piping hot to the public.

And when word finally got out, people stormed the bookstores for a taste.

In five years, Mark Victor Hansen and Jack Canfield's *Chicken Soup for the Soul* series has become an unprecedented publishing phenomenon. By January 2000, their publisher reported that they had sold an astounding forty-nine million books.[4] At least five Chicken Soup books were on the top-ten list of *Publisher's Weekly* paperback bestsellers simultaneously.[5]

These days, publishing whiz Mark Hansen is happy to report that thanks to Jack Canfield's invitation to lunch, he now has a monster success story to tell to his "How to *Mega* More Than Triple Your Income and Double Your Time Off" seminars.

YOU MIGHT LIKE TO KNOW

A portion of the proceeds of each of the Chicken Soup books is given to charity. Money from *Chicken Soup #1* was given to Literacy Volunteers. Eighty-five to 90 percent of Chicken Soup buyers are women. Mark Victor Hansen and Jack Canfield receive an average of one hundred unsolicited short stories a day for consideration for future Chicken Soup books. Staff writers cull these stories, then the two founding authors select the final 101 stories for each book. Patty Hansen and Georgia Canfield are equal owners with their husbands in Chicken Soup Enterprises. Mark Hansen was the recipient of the Horatio Alger Association of Distinguished Americans Award in Washington, D.C. Of their books Hansen said, "Our books go heart to heart, soul to soul to the core being of a person.... Our stories are so little, so bite-sized, that they don't intimidate people…they ignite the spirit."[6] Of future projects Hansen said, "My ideas keep having ideas. I have six thousand goals I want to accomplish in my lifetime."[7]

∞

A Penney Saved

*Many a time, a word of praise or thanks
or appreciation or cheer has kept a man on his feet.*
—WILLIAM BARCLAY

James's little pig business was going to have to go. The neighbors were complaining of disturbing snorts and disgusting smells. Eight-year-old James had gone into business after his father announced that he would have to start buying his own clothes, but now his father insisted that James shut down his business. "We can't take advantage of our neighbors," he said. James understood. And he never forgot the incident. From that point on, those words were the anchoring value in all his business ventures.

After high school in Missouri, James moved to Colorado, hoping the climate would benefit his ill health. While he was there, he opened a butcher shop. But when he refused to be bribed into giving bourbon in exchange for the business of a hotel chef, the chef got angry and spread false rumors that sank James in the meat business.

From Colorado, James traveled to Wyoming to work in a dry-goods store. He was such a great salesman that, before long, he had his own shop in a mining town and lived in a room above the store.

James was a conscientious and ethical businessman. Other merchants laughed at his cash-only, "Golden Rule" store, predicting he would fold in a matter of months. But in five years, James had surpassed them all and opened three more locations.

Business boomed. And during the next five years, he became the owner of thirty-four stores and was doing two million dollars a year in business. A short time later, he was so successful that he moved his headquarters to New York City and took the position of chairman of the board.

By 1917, James's store count was at fourteen hundred and climbing. Then suddenly, his whole world came crashing down on top of him.

His wife died unexpectedly while giving birth to their son, and James was devastated. For years, he wandered the streets of New York after work in search of a drink. Six years later, the stock market crashed, and James was ruined.

If anyone had reason to jump off the Empire State Building, James did. In a few agonizing seconds, James watched forty million dollars disappear from his personal bank account. And there was nothing he could do to stop it. In three years, he had lost everything he owned trying to pay his creditors.

Finally, mentally despondent and physically ill, James wound up in a sanatorium in Battle Creek, Michigan.

One morning, after he had been at the hospital for a while, James heard the sound of singing and decided to walk down the hall to locate the source. When he got to the door, he discovered that the employees were singing a hymn at the start of their day. James knew this hymn; his father had been a Baptist preacher. And as he sat listening in the back of the room, the words of the song washed over his soul: "Be not dismayed, whate'er betide, God will take care of you." Suddenly, unexplainably, James felt infused with light and hope. The song helped him feel God's love again and miraculously healed his shattered heart.

A short time later, fifty-six year old J. C. Penney was back at work, a brand-new man.

With renewed energy and drive, Penney borrowed money on his life-insurance policy and, over the next few years, began to regain a foothold in his old company. Before long, he was the talk of the town when he was again named chairman of the board.

By then the J. C. Penney Company had grown to fifty thousand employees nationwide, with each of them sharing in the company's profits. By 1951, there was a J. C. Penney store in every state in the nation, and sales reached more than one billion dollars.

Penney remained active in his company well into his eighties and died at the age of ninety-five. After Dr. Norman Vincent Peale spoke at his funeral, fifteen hundred people lifted their voices and sang in Penney's honor: "Be not dismayed whate'er betide, God will take care of you."

YOU MIGHT LIKE TO KNOW

At the age of eighty-four, J. C. Penney attended fifty-one store openings in twenty-four states, was a featured speaker more than one hundred times, and traveled more than sixty-two thousand miles visiting Penney stores and meeting customers. It was a coincidence that Penney's middle name was Cash. For many years, any

Penney's employee who used tobacco or drank liquor was fired. Once Penney was given a dessert with rum in the ingredients and said to a colleague, "That was liquor of some kind, wasn't it?" The man replied that he believed it was and said, "My doctor tells me that a little spot of whiskey is good for you." Penney replied, "Time to change doctors, I think."[8]

∞

How Ed Made a Mint

In God's providence, no person we meet is unimportant and no contact is casual.

—WARREN WEIRSBE

One day, a sharp, young advertising salesman named Ed Noble spotted a new kind of mint in a New York candy store. Its name and design intrigued him so much that he bought a pack and popped a mint in his mouth. Instantly, Ed loved the taste and was convinced the mint had incredible marketing potential. So he set off for Cleveland, Ohio, to sell the manufacturer on advertising through his company.

Unfortunately, when Ed approached Clarence Crane with his idea, the manufacturer wasn't the slightest bit interested in advertising. Crane was in the chocolate business. As far as he was concerned, the mints were just a small side item. He said, "The mint idea was just something to fill in during the summer when chocolate sales fall off."

But Ed had a feeling about these mints, and he was a determined salesman. He pressed Crane again. This time Crane gave a different response. He mentioned something Ed had not even remotely considered. The proposition would mark his life and become a defining moment in U.S. candymaking. Crane said, "If you think they're so great, why don't you buy the rights and make them yourself?"

Stunned by the offer, Ed gulped and asked Crane how much he wanted for the rights. Crane paused for a minute then said, "Five thousand dollars."

Ed had no business making mints. After all, he was a salesman, and he certainly didn't have five thousand dollars. But he sensed a rare opportunity that he couldn't pass up. Back in New York, Ed pitched the idea to his childhood friend J. Roy Allen, who agreed to put in fifteen hundred dollars of his own money. The two found more investors and managed to raise thirty-eight hundred dollars. Fortunately, by the time Ed Noble, J. Roy Allen, and Clarence Crane shook hands on the deal, the asking price had been reduced to twenty-nine hundred dollars, leaving the men nine hundred dollars to get their business rolling.

For the eager entrepreneurs, selling candy was anything but a piece of cake. The repeat business they'd been assured of suddenly evaporated. Faulty packaging spoiled the product. After a few weeks on the shelf, the mints lost their flavor and absorbed the smell of glue from their cardboard containers. As a result, none of the original merchants would risk placing a second order. Noble and Allen were forced to call on hundreds of new customers, switch to aluminum foil packaging, and do the tedious work of wrapping each package by hand.

But Ed believed in his product. He thought that if people just tasted his mints, they'd be sold on them. For the first year, Noble and Allen held down their day jobs while seeking new customers.

Their evenings were spent stuffing mints in sample bags for distribution on street corners and in building lobbies.

Then Ed hit on an idea that sent his business into orbit: counter merchandising. Ed knew mints, like chewing gum, were an impulse item. He designed display cartons for his mints and suggested to store owners that they "put them near the cash register with a price card. Then be sure every customer gets a nickel with his change."

It worked. Within a couple of years, Ed's five-cent mints made a quarter of a million dollars. And after thirteen years, J. Roy Allen cashed out his fifteen-hundred-dollar investment for a whopping three million dollars.

Clarence Crane's off-the-cuff remark to Ed Noble launched a legacy in American business. In fact, chances are pretty high that his comment, made in 1915, has, at one time or another, touched your life too.

Ever bought a pack of Life Savers?

YOU MIGHT LIKE TO KNOW

On an average day, about seventy-four miles of Life Saver rolls are made (one thousand rolls each minute). Currently there are thirty different flavors of Life Savers. The Pep-O-Mint flavor is still the number one bestseller. More than 120 million mints are made annually at the Holland, Michigan, manufacturing site. At least 55 percent of all Life Saver purchases are still unplanned.[9]

GOD'S WORD OF COMMERCE

Two are better than one, because they have a good return for their work.
—ECCLESIASTES 4:9

In our independence-driven culture, it is good to be challenged with the timeless principle of teamwork.

In the beginning, under the most perfect circumstances, God planned for the work of this world to be done in tandem. He called Adam and Eve as the first working team, with a mandate to cultivate the Garden of Eden and to subdue the earth. Even before sin entered the picture, God had ordained the couple to work in partnership.

Teams of artisans or family clans constructed all of the Old Testament tents, palaces, temples, and walls. Battles were fought with armies divided into teams. The disciples fished in teams. And when Jesus sent seventy disciples on their first mission trip, he sent them out in teams.

The vast majority of the commerce of the kingdom is done by people working together. Rare is success recorded by the lone man or woman. There is good reason for this.

The man or woman alone is more susceptible to attack. Think of Samson. "Though one may be overpowered, two can defend themselves" (Eccles. 4:12). The attack can be physical or mental. Either can more easily be avoided if others are standing by to help us defend ourselves.

Two heads are better than one. They think more creatively, cover more bases, remember more details, and generate more ideas.

Four arms are better than two. The work is accomplished sooner, with less stress and strain, if there are two or more at the task. And the man or woman who falls down can always get back up if he or she has a partner to reach down and give a hand.

With two, there can be singing and laughter and talking through the work, which can make an unpleasant job seem suddenly delightful.

And even though each team or couple needs a head, God has assured that no head can survive on its own without a body to which he is attached. And a leader is just a "nobody" until he has a group to follow him.

Even God is known to himself as the Trinity.

The Lord desires us to be happy, productive, safe, and cared for no matter what job we do or what task we attempt. And there appears to be no distinction between "spiritual " and "secular" work.

"Two are better than one, because they have a good return for their work"—God's formula for success, even in the twenty-first century.

BOOST YOUR OWN WORD POWER

Promote your fellow employees. Brag on their accomplishments. Boast about their contribution to the team. Purpose to hand out at least five genuine compliments a day. It is always the stronger person who can boost another up. Help a student start an after-school business. Encourage someone to take a night course to improve his or her skills. Offer to baby-sit his or her children during classes. Move out of your usual circle and network with new people in your field. Make every effort possible to get out of a job you dread. Change companies if you have to. A pay cut is only temporary when you are doing work you love. If you are doing work you love, you will be successful. If you are successful, you will see more rewards. Make a suggestion for your team at work to tackle a community-service project. You will be serving someone in need and building the camaraderie and momentum of your own team at the same time.

The sovereign Lord has given me an instructed tongue,
to know the word that sustains the weary.

—Isaiah 50:4

10

CHOICE WORDS OF COMPASSION

The Testament

You cannot do a kindness too soon,
for you never know how soon it will be too late.

—RALPH WALDO EMERSON

The man in the bed is sixty years old. He has called his young children in to tell them good-bye. He has been a patriot and a world-renowned writer, but his fame means nothing to him now. Taking the hands of his children, he asks his wife to read from the tattered New Testament lying beside him on the nightstand. He wants her to read the parable of the prodigal son. It is his favorite story of all. And he wants his children to hear it with him one last time.

The man's breathing is shallow, his eyes are clinched, and his thoughts lock on the pages the best they can while she reads. When the story is finished, he calls them close and says in a weakened voice, "My children, never forget what you have just heard. Have absolute faith in God and never despair of his pardon. I love you dearly, but my love is nothing compared with the love of God. Even if you should be so unhappy as to commit some dreadful crime, never despair of God. You are his children; humble yourselves before him, as before your father; implore his pardon, and he will rejoice over your repentance, as the father rejoiced over that of the prodigal son."

A few minutes later the man is dead.

In the days to come, his children will grieve, but not as those without hope. He had shown them how to live gloriously, and now he had shown them how to die gloriously.

The testament on the nightstand was once a gift. It had seen the man through years of frightful and harrowing circumstances, starvation, deprivation, and despair. And not a day went by since it was given to him that he failed to read something from it.

It was the giving of this book that gave him life.

The man had been born in Moscow. His parents had named him Fyodor. From a very young age, Fyodor's favorite pastime was reading. He especially loved the stories of Sir Walter Scott. In fact, it is said that the boy was so captivated by the experiences of Scott's characters that he would often faint, they seemed so real to him.

As a young man, Fyodor was concerned with social reform and joined a group of intellectuals who openly debated the great French theories of their day. To discuss these thoughts was forbidden in Russia, but Fyodor was young and idealistic and defiant of the czar's laws. One night a government informant crept into their meeting and had all thirty-three men arrested for conspiracy and sentenced to death.

So on a bone-chilling winter morning, the entire lot of them were marched to a scaffold, each wearing only a thin shroud. Coffins were piled nearby as the men listened to their funeral service in near-freezing temperatures. Facing them were soldiers armed with muskets, and when the time came for executions, the soldiers raised their guns to fire. But at the last moment a white flag appeared, meaning that the czar had decided to pardon the men. The whole charade had been a cruel joke planned by the czar to frighten them into submission. It worked in part. Some went crazy from the experience; others died soon after. And the rest were given ten years of exile in Siberia with the requirement of military service afterward.

On Christmas Eve, the prisoners' train departed. When it reached its destination, two women were there in the crowd to meet it. Someone must have sent them, but no one knows who. As the line of prisoners reached them, the women watched for their opportunity. As soon as the officers' backs were turned, one of the women slipped Fyodor a small New Testament, whispering for him to "search it carefully at his leisure."

Then the men moved on. The women disappeared, never to be heard from again.

When he opened the book later, Fyodor found twenty-five rubles—a practical, welcome gift, or a sign of more treasures to come?

Soon the testament was his closest companion in the most horrible of conditions. He later wrote, "Imagine an old crazy wood building that should have broken up as useless. In the summer it is unbearably hot, in the winter unbearably cold.... On the ground filth lies an inch thick: every instant one is in danger of slipping. The small windows are so frozen over that even by day one can scarcely read: the ice on the pane is three inches thick. We are packed like herrings in a barrel. The atmosphere is intolerable: the prisoners stink like pigs: there are vermin by the bushel: we sleep upon bare boards."

But it is in this rotting hell that Fyodor found Jesus Christ. The little New Testament guided him there as he studied the "precious volume" from one end to the other every moment he could. He memorized much of it and pondered its truths. The Word of God carried him through what would have killed most men.

In time, he walked among the prisoners and read the book aloud. They saw him as a prophet, gently rebuking their language, correcting their excesses, always speaking to them of poetry or science, of God and the love of his Son.

And in a letter from Siberia, he wrote, "One sees the truth more clearly when one is unhappy. And yet God gives me moments of perfect peace; in such moments I love and believe that I am loved.... I believe there is nothing lovelier, deeper, more sympathetic, more rational, more manly and more perfect than the Saviour."

Then finally in 1864, Fyodor was released from prison and sent to a garrison town near Mongolia to serve time as a common foot soldier.

Later, Fyodor and his brother published two monthly magazines. Ten years out of prison, he produced the first chapters of a book called *Notes from the Underground.* Then Fyodor's brother died, leaving him to fend for himself with the creditors. And in an effort to survive, he left Russia to live in Europe.

It was during this time in Europe that he wrote the famous epic *Crime and Punishment,* as well as *The Idiot* and *The Possessed.* And then when he finally returned to his homeland, Fyodor Dostoyevsky finished, not long before he died, what has been called the greatest novel of all time: *The Brothers Karamazov.*

On the morning of Dostoyevsky's funeral, forty thousand men marched with his coffin through the streets. Some of his students sent an open letter to his widow proclaiming, "Dostoyevsky's ideals will never be forgotten. From generation to generation we shall hand them down as a precious inheritance from our great and beloved teacher.... Dostoyevsky will always stand out brightly before us in the battle of life: for it was he who taught us the possibility of preserving the purity of the soul undefiled in every position of life and in all conceivable conditions."

After it was given to him, Fyodor Dostoyevsky was never very far from his Bible. It had seen him through countless desperations and had comforted him in darkness. It had accompanied him on his travels. At home, he kept it close in his writing table. He never made a major decision without consulting it. And on the day he died, it was with him there too.

YOU MIGHT LIKE TO KNOW

Dostoyevsky married his wife at the age of forty-five (she was nineteen) after she made it possible for him to meet a deadline for a publisher who had written in his contract that if Dostoyevsky failed to finish on time, he would forfeit all his royalties. Dostoyevsky was buried on their fifteenth wedding anniversary.

The monumental Russian writer Leo Tolstoy was alive in Dostoyevsky's time, though the two never met. He said, "When I heard of Dostoyevsky's death I felt that I had lost a kinsman, the closest and the dearest, and the one of whom I had the most need." Among his other difficulties, Dostoyevsky also suffered from epilepsy.

In the early seventies, theologian Malcolm Muggeridge learned that members of the Russian intellectual elite were finding renewal in Christianity. He asked one such member what he attributed this to, since no Christian literature, including the Bible, was permitted in their country. The man's reply was that the authorities had forgotten one thing: to ban the works of Dostoyevsky and Tolstoy, who wrote the most "perfect expositions of the Christian faith of modern times."[1]

∞

Stranger on the Sidewalk

*I expect to go through life but once. If therefore, there be any kindness
I can show or any good thing I can do for any fellow being,
let me do it now—as I shall not pass this way again.*

—WILLIAM PENN

Lorraine was twelve years old when she experienced what she would later call a turning point in her life.

One day while she was walking to the store, a nicely dressed woman stopped her on the sidewalk and said, "Honey, you're too big to have safety pins on your clothes."[2]

A button had come off Lorraine's jumper, and she was using a safety pin to hold it up. But why should this stranger care? Under normal conditions Lorraine might have been insulted or embarrassed, but the woman had such a kind, sweet spirit about her that Lorraine just stood there.

A small dime store was just down the street, and the woman asked if Lorraine would feel comfortable walking with her there. Lorraine said no. The woman seemed to understand and asked Lorraine if she would wait while she went to get something. Then she disappeared into the store.

Lorraine's family had little money. She and her brother lived with their mother, Clara, in Harlem. Her father had died when she was very young, so to make ends meet, her mother had gone out to get a job, putting her two children in day care. But Clara didn't like the arrangement; she could do a much better job of keeping her children herself. So she kept other people's children for two dollars a week. After a while, she became a licensed foster parent, and soon their five-room apartment was full of foster kids. Most of the children were from unwed mothers. Sometimes the children would cry, and Clara would tell Lorraine, "We have to make our home as comfortable as possible for them."[3]

Before it was over, Clara would care for more than forty foster children. And Lorraine would be their big sister. She would read to them, play with them, hold them, and love them. Having a house full of other people's children was normal for Lorraine. She thought everyone lived that way. Her family may not have had much money, but they did have tons of love.

A few minutes passed, and the nicely dressed woman returned to Lorraine, handing her a small box. Inside the box were spools of thread, buttons, and a couple of sewing needles. Lorraine was still speechless. The lady smiled and said again, "Honey, you are just too big to have safety pins in your clothes." Then the woman walked away.

Lorraine never saw the stranger again, but she never forgot what she did.

Many years later, as Lorraine sat in her car at a stoplight, she noticed a woman on the corner, slumped over on a crate. There was a bundle in her lap; Lorraine could see a tiny arm sticking out of the bundle. The woman was dozing off, and the baby she held was about to hit the ground. When the light changed, Lorraine drove past them, but then, about three blocks away, something told her to go back.

Maybe it was the memory of the lady on the sidewalk.

Gently shaking the woman, Lorraine handed her a piece of paper and told her if she needed help with her baby, she could take it to the address she had written on it. The address was her mother's apartment.

The next day the woman left her baby at Clara Hale's house. And as she did, the ministry of Hale House was born.

Today, more than thirty years later, more than three thousand babies of drug-addicted or HIV-positive mothers have received care at Hale House. They have come from police precincts, hospitals, welfare offices, pastors, social workers, relatives, and mothers who can no longer care for their babies.

For more than twenty of those thirty years, Mother Hale and her daughter, Dr. Lorraine Hale, worked together to secure the funds and oversee the children's care. Then in 1992, Mother Hale died, and her daughter has run with her legacy ever since.

At a recent fund-raising dinner for Hale House in New York, Dr. Hale said, "I'm not a professional, but I believe I qualify to help our children, as everybody's waiting for them to grow up and become what the Lord has intended them to be."[4]

Hale House is a temporary holding facility for children until their mothers can get help and resume care on their own. To help insure that the mothers make progress, Dr. Hale established Homeward Bound, a program that provides transitional housing and relapse prevention for former drug-addicted mothers and their children. It is a group home in which mothers live together with their children while getting ongoing support and counseling for their drug problems.

For a time, a separate home for mothers and children afflicted with the HIV virus was also established. But when the state required Hale House to administer the drug AZT, Dr. Hale declined, citing that between 50 to 70 percent of all the AIDS babies they had taken in since the eighties had lost all signs of the disease without medication. A home for terminally ill children was then founded as a result.

But Dr. Hale did not stop there.

She went on to sponsor Children Helping Children, a program designed to help troubled kids work at apprenticeships instead of receiving punishments for misdemeanor offenses. More than nine hundred children pass through the program each year. And the Time Out for Moms program began as a way of helping emotionally traumatized mothers reach out for help instead of hurting their children.

In order to keep Hale House functioning on the one-to-one, personal basis on which it was founded, the program receives no national, state, or city funding.

Of her amazing accomplishments, Dr. Lorraine Hale has said, "My mother's focus was that you've got to help other people in this world; otherwise why are you here?"[5]

YOU MIGHT LIKE TO KNOW

At a recent fund-raising banquet, Hale House raised more than six hundred thousand dollars. Their contributors have included baseball star Roberto Clemente, basketball star John Starks, Bill Cosby, Whitney Houston, M. C. Hammer, television weatherman Al Roker, and recording artist Lauryn Hill. Dr. Lorraine Hale has a Ph.D. in child development. Hale House recently established a Prayer Parent Program and has requested help from 150 Latino churches in New York City.[6] Ninety percent of all the children who have passed through Hale House have reunited with their mothers.[7]

∞

The Wild Man of Borneo

The simplest things give me ideas.
—JOAN MIRO (INVENTOR OF THE SNAP)

The circus had come to town, and like every other eight-year-old boy, George just had to get in on the action. Every act under the big top was a fascination to him, and he sat in wide-eyed wonderment while clowns, jugglers, fire-eaters, and lion tamers performed their feats in front of him. But there was one particular show that George could not stop thinking about.

Racing home, he described to his parents in vivid detail the colorful performers and daring high-wire stunts. Then he told them about the "Wild Man of Borneo" he had seen. Something about the wild man attracted him, and he asked his mother, "Are there any missionaries in Borneo telling the story of Jesus to the natives?"

His mother said no, that she did not believe there were any missionaries in Borneo. Her answer troubled George. He felt sorry that the people on that South Sea Island had gone all these years without God. And that very moment his eight-year-old heart determined that when he grew up, he would go to Borneo to tell the natives about Jesus.

George may have come by his missionary zeal quite naturally. His father had hoped to be a missionary to India, but circumstances did not allow him to follow his heart. But he told the dream to his children and prayed that one of his three boys would give his life for Christ in another land.

George was the answer to his prayers. In college, he studied the Bible and medicine and formed a prayer group that interceded regularly for Borneo. After graduation, he made the rounds of missions organizations, hoping one of them would agree to sponsor him. He tried a Presbyterian board, but they refused, saying they had no established work in Borneo. He approached the Christian and Missionary Alliance board, but no was the answer there too. Determined to get to Borneo, George then paid a personal visit to each man on the CMA board, asking him to reconsider. One of them suggested that he write a certain missionary who was working in China at that time, because he had expressed the same interest. This proved to be God's key for opening the way to Borneo.

Finally, a reply came from the missionary, saying that his group had been praying for someone to minister in Borneo. With the missionary's assistance, the board approved George's long-awaited appointment.

His first stop was at missionary school, where he learned the Low Malay language. When that was sufficiently accomplished, he set out to reach "the wild men" he had envisioned since childhood.

When George arrived in Borneo, he was so excited to be there that he jumped out of the boat and ran up to the first man he saw. Grabbing the man's hand, he shook it hard and claimed the man for Christ. Later George reflected, "When I reached the natives I felt like Joshua entering the Promised Land." Not long after this, the first native he had met gave his life to Christ, along with some of his neighbors.

Committed to the unreached people in the interior of the island, George traveled by boat and on foot for two hundred miles. To get there he and his group trekked along the treacherous Kajan River. During the journey, several men and supplies were lost to the raging rapids.

Then one day, in the midst of one of these trips, George saw something that gave him an idea that would revolutionize missionary travel.

He was sitting on a rock, exhausted from the strenuous work of lugging boats around the unnavigable sections of a river. Looking back, he could still see the campsite they had left earlier that morning and was disheartened by the miniscule progress they had made. It was now lunchtime, and as George and the porters were preparing the meal, he saw two great hornbill birds gliding over the river, soaring effortlessly across the gorge. Suddenly George had an idea and shouted, "Look! I'll do that!"

"You'll do what?" the porters asked staring at the birds overhead.

"I'll fly the gospel here, over the rapids, over the jungle, over the mountains."

The natives had never seen an airplane, so George had to explain what a "mechanical bird" looked like. Then, as they gave thanks for their food, George gathered the men on their knees to pray for a plane. It didn't even faze him that he didn't know how to fly one.

On his next furlough in the United States, George got his pilot's license. And on June 29, 1938, the first missions organization ever to use an airplane granted permission for George Fisk to take a Beechcraft SE 17B back to Borneo.

Getting the plane to Borneo was a stiff challenge. The distance was too great to fly it there, so they dismantled the plane piece by piece and shipped it over by boat. Men in the Dutch navy reassembled the plane once it arrived in Borneo, and specially trained mechanics kept it serviced. Special floats were installed so the plane could land on water. Finally, just as George predicted, his missionary plane carried the gospel into the air, over the rapids, over the jungle, and over the mountains of Borneo.

YOU MIGHT LIKE TO KNOW

While on furlough in the United States, George shared his vision of missionary aviation everywhere he went. One night after a presentation, Paul Robinson cornered George to talk further. Soon Paul was taking flying lessons and soloed for the first time just before the war broke out. But by the time the war was over, no mission agency would take Paul because he was over their age limit. Still believing in aviational mission work, he went before the board of trustees at Moody Bible Institute and presented statistics and figures on how much time and expense plane travel would save missionaries. The board liked the idea and approved a class called the "Missionary Technical Course."

Later George met James Truxton, and the two of them, along with two other former military pilots, launched what is now called Mission Aviation Fellowship. Later groups like Wycliffe Bible Translators, Sudan Interior Mission, and Jungle Aviation and Radio Service were also launched, thanks to the vision and determination of George Fisk. Moody Aviation, the organization started by George's friend Paul Robinson, is now responsible for training at least half of all the missionary pilots, mechanics, and radio technicians in the world.[8]

∞

How a Dying Buddhist Found Life

You who are as little children in God's church,
you who do not know much, but try to tell others what little you know.
If it be the same gospel truth, and be blessed by the same Spirit,
it will not matter to the souls who are blessed by you whether they were
converted or comforted under a person of one or ten talents.

—CHARLES SPURGEON

The Korean Conflict was over, but like many of his country-men, Yonggi was barely scraping by. At seventeen, he was a hard worker and carried several jobs a day, including a job as a tutor. One day, during a tutoring session, Yonggi became violently ill.

Without warning, blood began to gush from the young man's mouth and nose. He could do nothing to stop it. Within minutes, his chest and stomach were filled with blood, and he passed out. When he regained consciousness, he was weak and severely shaken but somehow managed to make it home.

Selling whatever possessions they could, Yonggi's parents col-lected enough money to take him to a hospital for tests. When the doctors finished examining him, the news was devastating: aggres-sive tuberculosis. The doctors were definite. His was a very unusual, rapidly spreading form of the disease for which there was no cure.

"You have three, at the most four, months to live," one doctor said. "Go home, young man. Eat anything you want. Say good-bye to your friends."

Dazed and depressed, Yonggi walked the streets of Seoul, passing hundreds of Korean refugees displaced by the war. He identified with their utter hopelessness.

A practicing Buddhist, Yonggi prayed daily that Buddha would help him. But no help came. As the weeks passed, his condition only worsened. He hung a three-month calendar on the wall and waited to die.

Then one day he got a visit from a high-school girl who came to talk to him about Christ. She explained about Christ's virgin birth, death on a cross, and resurrection. Yonggi was unfazed by her "stories" and felt relieved when she left.

The girl came again the next day and the next, always sitting by his bed and talking about Christ. Finally, Yonggi had enough and yelled at her for annoying him. Instead of running away or shouting back, the girl dropped to her knees and prayed. Tears fell down her cheeks as she cried out for Yonggi's soul. This deeply touched him. Hers was more than mere talk. She had love and compassion, a radical contrast to his Buddhist rituals and philosophies.

Yonggi apologized and then said, "Please don't cry. I now know about your Christian love. Since I am dying, I will become a Christian for you."

The girl was overjoyed. She praised God, shook his hand, and gave him a Bible. And as she did, the girl spoke the words that would usher Yonggi Cho into the kingdom of God.

"Search the Bible," she said. "If you read it faithfully, you will find the words of life."

It was the first time Yonggi had ever held a Bible. In his weakened condition, it was a struggle for him even to open it. He turned to the beginning of the book, but the girl smiled and said, "Sir, you are so sick that if you start at Genesis, I don't think you will last long enough to finish Revelation. If you start from the Book of Matthew, you will have enough time."

As Yonggi read the Bible, he kept seeing references to Jesus Christ, the Son of God. He was so near death that he craved something greater than the stoic principles of his religion. He knew he needed a God who could share in his struggles and suffering, a God who could help him overcome them.

He discovered that Christ loved sinners while still hating sin. He saw that Christ healed the sick, which brought him hope that he might also be healed. And he learned that Christ gave peace to the troubled, raised the dead, and had compassion on the demon-possessed.

When he finished reading the New Testament, Yonggi became convinced that Jesus Christ was real. He knelt down and asked Christ into his heart to save him, heal him, and deliver him from death.

Immediately he felt changed. For the first time, joy and peace poured over him, and he stood up and shouted, "Glory be to the Lord!"[9]

From that day on Yonggi devoured the Bible. It energized his faith. Despite his impending doom, he was no longer afraid. Eventually, he began to believe that he would not die. And six months later, he felt well enough to get out of bed.

In 1958, Yonggi Cho graduated from an Assembly of God Bible school and began a tent church outside the city of Seoul with the help of his future mother-in-law and a missionary. Within six years, the church had grown to nearly two thousand people.

Then one day Yonggi collapsed during a service. His strength had never fully returned after his illness, and he considered resigning from his booming congregation. But during his recovery, he once again found help in the Scriptures. After reading Exodus 18:13–26, he discovered that Moses' solution for handling the stress of a large congregation was to divide them into groups. This gave Yonggi an idea that probably saved his life and eventually led hundreds of thousands of South Koreans to Christ—a church made of "cell" groups. He insisted that the focus of the church move to small groups, led by qualified pastors, who would meet in homes and apartments all over the city during the week. To say it worked is an understatement.

By 1982, the church had grown so large that it had already spawned nearly one hundred daughter churches—one with five thousand members and another with three thousand members—and more than one hundred full-time, seminary-trained missionaries had been sent to North and South America, Europe and other parts of Asia.

The persistent high-school girl who prayed for Yonggi Cho thought she was merely extending the compassion of Christ to a dying man. She had no idea that God had chosen her to capture the heart of one the greatest Christian servants in the twentieth century, bringing new life to millions!

Ultimately, Dr. David Yonggi Cho's Yoido Full Gospel Church in Seoul, South Korea, became the largest Protestant church in the world. By 1992, it had reached an astonishing seven hundred thousand members.

YOU MIGHT LIKE TO KNOW

In 1996, Dr. Cho was honored by his church for forty years of ministry. The South Korean deputy prime minister and a former prime minister were in attendance. The Guinness Book of World

Records has listed Yoido Full Gospel Church as the world's largest church. In the mid-eighties, Yoido Full Gospel Church employed more than two thousand full-time pastors and workers and conducted seven services each Sunday. At that time, each service in the main auditorium, in addition to their side chapels, held thirty thousand people.[10]

GOD'S WORD OF COMPASSION

Our God is full of compassion.
—Psalm 116:5

It is sometimes difficult for us to straddle the contrast been the Almighty, all-powerful God and the "softer side" of the Savior. And though down here the perfect blend is rare to see, we need to remind ourselves that Jesus is the complete package.

It was God's compassion that clothed the first sinners with skins. It was his compassion that saved Lot at Sodom. And it was his compassion that called Christ to the rescue. He has been here. He knows what it is like here. He has seen what we must endure.

God knows our frame. He has compassion on our frail humanity. He knows what it is like to be human, yet he never holds it against us. He sees the conditions that we live in, and he has pity on our spiritual poverty.

God knows our failures. He has seen us stranded on the side of the road, and he has picked us up and carried us back for help. He has seen us hungry and not withheld bread, though we've squandered our own precious wedding feast.

God knows our forgetfulness. He knows we like trinkets that tantalize us, even though we have keys to the kingdom vault.

At times we are obstinate people—denying his presence and resisting his protection. But he is patient. And though we come dragging home, whipped and beaten from our date with the world, he wipes our tears and soothes our temper without ever saying, "I told you so."

Christ sees us lying in the gutter of our own doing and still takes us home to his family.

The Mighty Lord is a skillful potter, aware of our earthly tendencies to crack under pressure. And yet he is compassionate.

Now—if we could just learn to be like that.

BOOST YOUR OWN WORD POWER

Rate your capacity for compassion on a scale of one to ten. Then ask a friend to rate you. Then ask God to rate you. Average all three. What do you think is keeping you from a higher score? How can you shift to a higher gear? Pray to see with your heart. Who do you know with a gift of compassion? Ask questions. Learn what makes them tick. Ask when they first felt merciful and caring toward others. Ask how they deal with the stress of it.

Put your compassion into action. Offer a genuine listening ear. Check around home and church first. It is often easier to show compassion to strangers than to people we already know. This should not be so. Offer to pray for people you see in obvious crisis—a car accident, a wayward child, or a lost job. Start a care group for people who need support for addictions or recovery issues. Do you know someone who could use a visit?

Do more little acts of compassion. When someone cuts in front of you on the highway or in line, imagine what circumstance may have pushed them to do it and let them through. Put yourself in their shoes. Next time, let someone else have the parking space you saw first. Write a note to an overwhelmed teacher, administrator, physician, or Realtor. At a moment he or she least expects it, pardon a child from discipline for a poor grade or unacceptable behavior. Remember what it feels like to fail. Show them God's mercy. Get involved in people's lives. Ask Christ to give you a "heart transplant."

Naphtali is a doe let loose,
He gives beautiful words.

—GENESIS 49:21 NASB

11

CHOICE WORDS OF CONFIDENCE

The Greatest Library Find

The power of printed words to alter lives is phenomenal.
—MERRILL DOUGLASS

It is four weeks until Christmas, but you would never know it in this neighborhood. A putrid odor crawls up from the gutters and into the street. The soggy slush that once was snow is now littered with trash. Bars and peep shows line the block. The street is deserted—except for a thin, tattered man peering through the window of a pawnshop.

The man is a bum. His teeth chatter, and his long, greasy hair dangles at his shoulders. His beard smashed against the glass, his bloodshot eyes graze the contents on the shelf until they land on a small metal object—a handgun. He stares at it. From the window he can read the price tag: twenty-nine dollars.

He can buy that handgun. He can buy that gun, take it back to his two-bit excuse for a room, and pull the trigger. The man stuffs his hands in his pocket and finds three crumpled up ten-dollar bills. He thinks he could do it. He wants to do it. But he doesn't. He doesn't have the guts.

The man was not born a bum. His father was an Italian immigrant who worked as a gardener to put food on the table, and his mother was a spunky Irish woman who told him repeatedly in childhood that he would be a great writer.

As a boy, the man loved reading and wrote stories for amusement. In high school, he worked on the school paper and planned to study journalism at the University of Missouri. But his mother died the summer after high-school graduation, and he ended up as a bombardier in the air force.

The man had a successful military career, so he came back from the war in 1945 believing he could do just about anything. He went to New York City and set up shop as a writer, but after six months of knocking on the doors of more than fifty magazine companies, the man went home to Boston. Before long he got a job, found a wife, and settled into a house he purchased on the GI Bill. And for the next ten years, the man did the best he could to make ends meet and stay one step ahead of his creditors.

One night, after failing to close an insurance deal, the man walked into a bar. He needed a drink after the day he had had. Soon he was stopping by the bar every night and coming home drunk. This went on for months, until his wife could no longer stand it. She took their daughter and left.

With no one to stop him, the man drank even more, until he lost his job and, eventually, his home. Finally he was forced to pack up his few clothes, get in his car, and drive out of town.

The man worked his way across the country. He drove oil trucks in Texas, did construction in Oklahoma, and set bowling pins in

California. At thirty-five, he was even a busboy at a Howard Johnson's.

Finally, the man ended up in Cleveland, where he spent several
nights in drunk tanks then walked the streets. That's when he saw
the gun in the window. That's when he thought of killing himself.
But he couldn't go through with it.

Later that day, the man walked into the only warm, dry place
open to him at the time, the public library. He liked books, thanks
to his mother, so he began to spend every day at the library, wondering where he had gone wrong and searching for answers.

Over time, the man picked up odd jobs and drove back east,
still stopping by the libraries as much as he could. He read Aristotle, Norman Vincent Peale, Ralph Waldo Emerson, Benjamin
Franklin, and Dale Carnegie. In time, the man discovered that the
more he read, the less he wanted a drink. Eventually, his alcoholism dwindled down to only an occasional beer.

The man's self-esteem slowly grew. He even bought some new
clothes. But he still didn't have a steady job. That's why he had
time on his hands that day. That's why Og Mandino was sitting at
the main library in Concord, New Hampshire, the morning his
whole life changed.

There was a book in the library that day, one that Og hadn't
seen before. It was different from other books he had read, ones
that promised personal miracles in thirty days or less. This book
was called *Success through a Positive Mental Attitude* by W. Clement
Stone and Napolean Hill. In the book, Og found a phrase that
nearly jumped off the page when he read it. This phrase contained
an insight that shed light on his suffering and pointed the way out
of poverty: "You can accomplish anything you wish that is not

contradictory to the laws of God or man, providing you are willing to pay the price."

"Pay the price." That was it. Seems simple enough, yet Og had
not been willing to do this. He finally saw that there would be no
quick fix to success and that, in order for good things to happen to
him, he would have to invest in himself.

Og devoured the book. He read it and reread it countless times.
When his courage was at its strongest, he traveled to Boston and
applied for a job as a salesman at W. Clement Stone's New England
company, Hearthstone Insurance. To Og's surprise, they hired him.
Soon he was making more money in a week than he had made in
his life.

In a year, Og became a sales manager. In an effort to encourage
his salesmen, he rented a typewriter and wrote a sales manual that
incorporated some of W. Clement Stone's principles of success. Og
mailed the manual to the home office in Chicago; they liked it so
much that they offered him a job writing in their sales-promotion
department.

This led to his being the editor of *Success Unlimited,* a magazine
started by Napolean Hill and W. Clement Stone as an in-house
motivational publication. One month, in the early stages of Og's
editorship, the magazine came up short for an article. Realizing
that they would have to meet the deadline, Og stayed up all night
writing a piece on the golfer Ben Hogan, who had come back from
a near fatal car accident to win a major golf tournament.

One day, a New York publisher was sitting in the dentist's office
and happened to read Og's article. The publisher was so impressed
that he wrote Og a letter offering to look at any book material he
might have. So Og Mandino went to work and wrote a little book

called *The Greatest Salesman in the World*. The rest is publishing history.

Within four years, *The Greatest Salesman in the World* had sold 350,000 hardcover copies. In 1973, Bantam Books became interested in buying it, and they flew Og to New York to look him over. For more than an hour, he answered questions and discussed plans for future books. Then the chairman of Bantam, Oscar Dystel, got up, extended his hand, and said, "Congratulations, Og, we've just bought your book."

Anxious to get to a phone to tell his wife, Og ran out to the street. Just then a thunderstorm hit, so he raced to the nearest opened door and ducked inside. It was a church. Overwhelmed and grateful, Og walked to the front of the church, got on his knees, and cried. Then he lifted his head and said, "Mom, wherever you are, I want you to know...we made it!"

Og Mandino became one of the foremost inspirational and self-help authors in the world. He wrote seventeen books that, by 1990, had sold more than twenty-five million copies in eighteen languages.[1]

YOU MIGHT LIKE TO KNOW

Thousands of people have credited Og Mandino's books with turning their lives around. Actor Matthew McConaughey (*A Time to Kill*) has attributed his success to repeated readings of *The Greatest Salesman in the World*.

Even though the book was first written in 1968, it still sells approximately seventy-five hundred copies every month. Other books by Og Mandino include *The Christ Commission* and *The Greatest Miracle in the World*.[2] Of the authors he read in the library,

Og said, "I read their words with an open mind and a burning desire to change…and I had nothing to lose by accepting their principles and applying them to a life that had been wasted up to that time. I owe them so very much and in every book I write I am still trying to repay my debt."[3]

∞

Two Jacks Serve an Ace

God builds his kingdom primarily through ordinary people who are willing to use daily encounters to tell others about the salvation that is available in Jesus Christ.

—TONY CAMPOLO

Stan was playing in a four-day tennis tournament in Arizona when he met Jack, one of the tournament organizers. Stan's team had traveled from the University of Southern California, and while they were in Arizona, Jack, an insurance man by trade, took a special interest in Stan. He invited Stan to dinner, took him to church with him, then offered Stan a book and said, "Here's something you might like to read sometime. It's stories of famous professional athletes and how they view their faith. I think you'll find it interesting."

Stan thanked Jack for his hospitality, took the book, and said that he'd read it as soon as he got the chance.

On the trip back to school, Stan pulled the book out and leafed through the pages. He recognized the names of many players and was surprised to read how serious they were about their faith. Stan read page after page of testimonies from some of the world's greatest athletes and was struck by their perspectives concerning their sports. As good as these athletes were, their relationships with Christ were clearly more important to them. And after reading the book, Stan felt challenged to evaluate his own spiritual values. He had to admit, "If I died in a car accident today, tennis would have been all I had ever lived for."[4]

During this same time, an athletes' Bible study was being launched on the USC campus. Each week, Don Williams, the youth pastor from the Hollywood Presbyterian Church, came over to the athletic dorm to lead the study. One day, a guy from the study invited Stan to join them. Stan was ripe for the group but had several major questions about Christianity. Each week, as he sat in with the guys, Don was patient to help Stan work through his doubts. As a kid, Stan had gone to church with his parents, but religion had never meant much to him. Once he even duped his parents into believing he was sitting in church when he had really slipped across the street to see a movie.

But finally, one night when he was by himself in his dorm room, Stan was ready for something other than tennis to be the Lord of his life. He prayed and asked Christ to be his Lord and Savior.

About this time, Stan's singles and doubles games began to take off. In 1967, he won the NCAA doubles title with his good friend Bob Lutz, then in 1968, he took both the NCAA singles and doubles titles.

Before long, Stan was traveling the world, hoping to make his mark as a professional tennis player. He knew he was good, but just how good? The competition was tough, and there were a whole host of champions to beat.

One of those champions was the Spanish tennis star Pancho Gonzales.

In 1971, Stan made it to the finals of a tournament at London's

Wimbley Stadium, only to find himself staring across the net at none other than Pancho Gonzales. Even though Stan played well against him that day, he just couldn't pull out the win.

Dejected and discouraged at the loss, Stan walked off the court and, a few minutes later, looked up to see American tennis legend Jack Krammer walking toward him. Anyone within a thousand miles of a tennis ball knew who Jack Krammer was. Both Stan and Jack hailed from southern California, and Stan had grown up hearing all about him.

"Kid, you are playing really well," Jack said, pulling the young rookie aside. "Keep it up, and I believe you have what it takes to be one of the best players in the world."[5]

Stan could tell Jack really meant what he said. If Jack Krammer thought he was good, well, there must be something to it. This was the greatest compliment Stan had ever received, and it was the turning point in his tennis career. From that moment on, Stan's sagging confidence leapt to the next level.

Within hours, Stan was winning every game he played. There was still a doubles match to play at Wimbley, and Stan captured it. Then the tour moved on to the Stockholm Open, where he took both the singles and doubles titles. Then he flew to Japan for the Grand Prix Masters Tournament, where he placed in the finals on his twenty-third birthday. And that night there was cause for double celebration because Stan had astounded everyone by winning that prestigious tournament too!

Another "gift" Stan received that year on his birthday was his draft notice. The Vietnam War was still going strong, and Stan's number had come up. Right away, he was commanded to report to the army in Los Angeles. But after completing basic training, Stan was not shipped to the battlefield; instead, he was given the honor of serving his country on the tennis court. His immediate duty was to win the international Davis Cup championship for America. And of the twenty-four matches Stan played in the Davis Cup, he won twenty-two.

But the best was yet to come.

With Jack Krammer's words still fresh in his ears, soldier Stan Smith went on to become the number one men's tennis player in the world by winning both the U.S. Open in 1971 and Wimbledon in 1972.

YOU MIGHT LIKE TO KNOW

Throughout Stan Smith's illustrious tennis career, he has remained a committed Christian man, husband, and father. At the height of his career, Stan was spiritually mentored by Eddie Waxer, a Campus Crusade for Christ staff member who traveled across Europe with the expressed intent of discipling Stan and other professional athletes.

In his career, Stan has won thirty-nine singles titles, sixty-one doubles titles (with Bob Lutz), and represented America in the Davis Cup ten times. America won the Davis Cup seven of those years, and Stan was responsible for winning the final point to clinch the cup five straight times. Stan Smith and Bob Lutz rank as the only team in tennis history to win U.S. national titles on grass, clay, hardcourt, and indoor surfaces. Stan has won the thirty-five-and-over singles title both at Wimbledon (1984 and 1985) and at the U.S. Open in 1984. He also won the thirty-five-and-over doubles title at Wimbledon (1991 and 1992) with Peter Fleming. Stan was inducted into the International Tennis Hall of Fame in 1987, the halls of fame for USC and the state of South Carolina, and the Collegiate Tennis Hall of Fame. He has also served as the director of coaching for the United States Tennis Association since 1988.

Stan is the author of *It's More Than Just a Game* and has one of the longest running shoe contracts ever with Adidas. In his book, *Days of Grace*, the late Arthur Ashe told an interesting story. One day, he and Stan were at a controversial championship point. The umpire was unsure if Smith had won the point or not. Ashe looked over and simply asked Smith if he had gotten the ball. When Stan said that he had, Ashe gave him the point and conceded the championship. Later Ashe told reporters, "Believe me, I am no fool. I wouldn't take anybody's word for it. But if Stan Smith says he got to the ball, he got it. I trust his character."

∞

A Glorious Enterprise

If you want to change the world, pick up your pen.
—MARTIN LUTHER

There was never a time when a letter was more needed. William was in the fight of his life, and it seemed as if all hell had rallied against him. But there were a few on his side, a chosen few whose support gave him the strength to persevere against great odds.

William Wilberforce was a member of the British parliament, but more significant in his eyes was his calling as a child of God. He was converted to Christ in 1785 while touring Europe with a minister friend who was a part of the ever-growing evangelical movement. As a new believer, William was seized with the shallowness of his life and wanted to leave politics. However he remained in office, due to the counsel of John Newton, a man who had once been a ruthless slave trader but was now an evangelical clergyman. Newton's counsel to William was firm: He must remain in public life and use his political career to further the cause of Christ.

Taking Newton's advice, William went to work with great conviction.

In 1787, he influenced the prime minister and the king of England to issue a proclamation urging magistrates to enforce existing legislation against drunkenness, blasphemy, and other misdemeanors. And he criticized the social elite for "possessing only the veneer of Christian belief" but not the real thing in a book called *A Practical View of the Prevailing Religious Systems of Professed Christians*. It sold more than seventy-five hundred copies in six months and ignited a serious spiritual awakening in the upper classes of Britain.[6]

For twenty years, powerful merchants and slave traders fought against William as he battled to abolish the slave trade in the House of Commons. William knew he had a mandate from God. And though opposition was strong, he held on.

One of the events that enabled him to endure was a letter he received from his good friend John Wesley, founder of the Methodist Church. Wesley was eighty-eight years old, and this was one of the last letters he ever wrote. Wesley's parting words to William, written February 1791, were these:

Dear Sir:

Unless the divine power has raised you up...I see not how you can go through with your glorious enterprise, in opposing that execrable villainy, which is the scandal of religion, of

England, and of human nature. Unless God has raised you up for this very thing, you will be worn out by the opposition of men and devils. But "if God be for you, who can be against you?" Are all of them stronger than God? O "be not weary in well doing!" Go on in the name of God and in the power of his might, till even American slavery, (the vilest that ever saw sun) shall vanish away before it... That He who has guided you from your youth up, may continue to strengthen you in this and all things, is the prayer of,

Your affectionate servant,

J. Wesley[7]

For many years after he received the letter, William Wilberforce fought the battle against slavery to no avail. But at key times throughout the years, he reread that note to boost his confidence and resolve.

Sixteen years later, in 1807, it became officially illegal to purchase slaves in Britain. This was a much-celebrated victory, but William soon discovered that halting the trade and wiping out slavery completely were two different things. He spent the next twenty-six years of his life working to abolish slavery entirely.

Finally, just before he died, William heard the news: Parliament had passed a bill to abolish slavery.

Though he had been ridiculed for his faith and his defense of slaves, William Wilberforce was buried in Westminster Abbey with an epitaph that read:

Eminent as he was in every department of public labour,
And a leader in every work of charity...His name will ever
    be specially

Identified with those exertions which, by the blessing of God, removed from

England the guilt of the African slave trade, and prepared the way for the

abolition of slavery in every colony of the Empire.[8]

YOU MIGHT LIKE TO KNOW

The abolition of slavery in Britain directly led to the same in America. Wilberforce dedicated his life to many humanitarian causes. In 1802, he organized the Society for the Suppression of Vice, lobbied for more humane laws for prisoners, and took part in other evangelical activities to improve the social climate of his day. John Newton, the ex-slave trader who encouraged Wilberforce to remain in public office, was the author of the hymn "Amazing Grace."

∞

I See Something in You

The applause of a single human being is of great consequence.
—SAMUEL JOHNSON

James was proud of his new Winchester rifle. He and a friend had already given it some target practice. Now he was itching for a chance to take it hunting. Most guys James knew went hunting with their dads, but he wasn't counting on his dad for that. His dad was hardly ever home, and when he was, he'd be in no shape to hold a gun.

And that's the way it was the night James's dad burst through the door. The man was drunk again and raging mad for no apparent reason. He wanted to hurt somebody, and James was the first person he saw. His dad was going to beat him up, he said, maybe kill him if he felt like it, so James ran to his room. His heart pounding, James grabbed a baseball bat and thought, *If he follows me I'm going to crush him.* He could still hear his dad yelling in the living room. Then James remembered his rifle.

He ran to the closet and shoved in a cartridge. Then with as much courage as he could muster, he walked back in the living room, pointed the gun at his dad's chest, and said, "If you so much as move your hand, I'm going to blow a hole in you big enough for somebody to crawl through!"

James had seen the marks on his mother's face and neck from the last time his dad was like this. His mom had said that if she hadn't passed out on the floor that night, her husband would have killed her for sure. James remembered her fear. And he stood poised to pull the trigger.

James's father shouted and cursed as he reached for the phone to call the police. And a few minutes later, he was still yelling as the squad car carted him off to jail for some time on unrelated charges.

The relationship between James and his father had always been a frightening one. Growing up, James didn't know what to think of his dad half the time. It wasn't until he was ten years old that his father had come to live with them.

James had been born in the charity ward of a Houston, Texas, hospital. His mother was a forty-year-old practical nurse when she became pregnant after being sexually assaulted by the son of a man she was caring for. At first she considered an abortion, but her doctor refused to perform it. So she carried her child to term. When he was born, she placed an ad in the paper that read: *Wanted—Loving Christian couple to raise newborn boy. References required.*

Katie Bell Hale, a Southern Baptist pastor's wife, saw the ad and immediately rushed down to the hospital. Her husband was away on a hunting trip, and she didn't have time to tell him the news. So when he returned that day, there was a newborn baby in the house.

For the next five years, the Hales cared for little James as if he were their son. Often they begged James's mother to let them adopt him, but she just couldn't do it. From time to time, James's mom showed up to visit the boy. Then, one day, she showed up to take him back.

The Hales were beside themselves with grief. They cried to the point of exhaustion as James's mother led him down the driveway with a little suitcase in his hand. They had poured their whole lives into the child, and now he was being snatched away.

For the next five years or so, James and his mother wandered from place to place, never staying anywhere for more than six months. His father was out of the picture, but once, when James was sick and his mother thought he was dying, she called his dad and said, "Joe, if you want to see your son, you'd better come see him now." And when he finally showed up to meet James, he drove up over the curb and walked in drunk.

A few years later, for reasons James didn't understand, his parents got married and his dad came to live with them for the first time. At first James thought, *Wow! I've got a daddy.* But he was soon to learn that this man had no concept or capacity for fatherhood.

When his dad was out of drinking money, he would steal the money James had in his little savings bank. Sometimes James would discover that his hair tonic was gone and realize that his father had drunk that too. His dad daily cursed at James and raged at him in anger. James never knew what shape he'd be in when he saw him.

The incident with the gun was the last straw for James. With his father in prison and his mother's life a wreck, James decided to pack his bags and move back to Pasadena with the Hales.

The Wednesday night after James arrived, the Hales brought him to the church where Mr. Hale was the pastor. After a time of singing, Mr. Hale invited the youth in the church to come to the front and give testimonies about what Christ had done in their lives. James was skeptical, knowing how his buddies back home would handle this. But one by one, sharp-looking, excited teenagers got up and talked about how they loved God, how Jesus was real in their lives, and how he'd helped them with their problems. Some even talked about God being their father. The more they talked, the more James felt a lump growing in his throat. All through Mr. Hale's sermon, James thought about what they had said. As they stood to sing the closing hymn, Mr. Hale said, "If you want to give your life to God tonight, come take my hand."

James wanted to do this. He was desperate to do it, but he was fearful and shy in public. He didn't want to walk forward. He grabbed hold of the pew in front of him and squeezed it hard.

Then he looked up and saw Mrs. Hale walking toward him with tears in her eyes. She was crying for him, and the sight of her melted his heart. She put her hand on James's shoulder and asked, "James, don't you want to go to Jesus?"

"Yes, ma'am, but I'm afraid," he said.

"I'll go with you, James. We could go together."

And with that he slowly stepped out into the aisle and walked forward to put his life in the hands of God.

A year or so later, James was in another service when he heard God speak to his heart about his future. He heard God say, "James, I'm calling you to preach. I want you to become an evangelist."[9] But James was shy and insecure in public. He could hardly give a book report in school, much less preach to an audience. That same night after the service, an excited but apprehensive James went up to one of the church deacons and asked him if he thought God could use him to preach. The deacon looked squarely at James and said, "Honestly, son, no. Not to preach."[10]

But if James was ever sure of anything, he was sure he had heard God on this. And he set about the task of getting ready.

James headed to East Texas Baptist College. He was bold about his faith and eager for the guys on campus to like him. But the guys in the dorm cracked jokes about him and laughed at his calling to preach.

All except one guy.

One night when James was a freshman, he heard a knock on his door and in walked an upperclassman named Billy Foote. Billy had been watching James and noticed the difficulties he was having fitting in. He had been thinking about it for a while and had something to say to him. He walked over to James, put his hand on his shoulder, and said, "James, I want to tell you something. I see something in you that I don't see in those other boys who are making fun of you. And I just wanted to come up here and tell you that."

To some, this comment wouldn't have meant much. But to James Robison, they were the sweetest words he had ever heard. For the first time in his life, someone believed in him, thought he was special, and saw his potential. For the first time, someone saw something good in him and said so to his face.

To the shock and surprise of almost everyone, James Robison was soon conducting citywide crusades in large cities all across the country. He spoke in high schools during the day then watched as thousands streamed into football stadiums and coliseums at night. He could hardly keep up with the demands of being one of the most dynamic young Southern Baptist preachers.

James often prayed that God would touch his father's life and heal him. One night, he invited his dad to hear him speak at a meeting that was being held near his father's home. But when James arrived to pick him up, the old man had changed his mind and decided not to go. For James this was one more disappointment in a long jagged line of heartaches with his dad. Sadly, his father died not long after this.

Eventually James became acquainted with Billy Graham, who encouraged him to start a television ministry in 1971. And when he did, thousands more received Christ.

Then in 1992, James changed the name of his organization from the James Robison Evangelistic Association to LIFE Outreach International because he wanted the ministry to be purpose-driven instead of person-centered. His television show took on a new interactive format, and he began to interview guests like Governor George W. Bush, Bishop T. D. Jakes, Robert Duvall, Kathie Lee Gifford, and Zig Ziglar. Today, James's wife, Betty, cohosts the show with him. The program reaches into one hundred million households in the United States and Canada.

Much of James's ministry is now focused in other parts of the world. Each month LIFE Outreach helps feed more than one hundred thousand children throughout Africa. It houses five hundred orphans in Rwanda and provides schooling, medical care, a fruit and vegetable farm, and a food-processing plant in Mozambique. And it is estimated that more than four million Africans have accepted Christ as a result of the LIFE Outreach-sponsored crusades that began in 1993.[11]

In the acknowledgments of his 1997 book *My Father's Face*, James Robison wrote a note to his good friend and dream booster Billy Foote. It said, "Thanks to Billy Foote, the best man at my wedding, who in college saw me as a freshman and said, 'I see something in you I don't see in others.' He gave me a chance and helped launch a ministry that has reached to the ends of the earth. It was because of the confidence Billy expressed to me that I gained a much-needed confidence in the Lord."[12]

YOU MIGHT LIKE TO KNOW

In five hundred of his early crusades, James Robison ministered to more than fifteen million people, with more than one million indicating a decision to receive Christ. LIFE Outreach also sponsors orphanages in China and Romania and spreads the gospel by film throughout India. Presently the ministry has outreaches in twenty foreign countries and has a vision to establish effective mission life in every population center in the world.

James is the author of more than a dozen books, including *My Father's Face*, *Thank God, I'm Free*, *Sex Is Not Love*, and *Knowing God as Father*. He and his wife, Betty, are the parents of three children and eleven grandchildren.

One night a young man was nearly dragged by a high-school friend to a James Robison crusade in East Texas. He was a country boy whose father was a bootlegger. He lived a godless life in a run-down, shacklike house. But by the end of the night, young Clark Whitten gave his heart to Christ. Today Clark leads the thirty-five-hundred-member Calvary Assembly of God Church in Orlando, Florida—just one life that was touched by the power of God through James Robison.

GOD'S WORD OF CONFIDENCE TO YOU

Is not the LORD your God with you?
And has he not granted you rest on every side?…
Now devote your heart and soul to seeking the LORD your God.
—1 CHRONICLES 22:18–19

Our God will fight for us!
—NEHEMIAH 4:20

When I felt secure, I said, "I will never be shaken." O LORD, when you
favored me, you made my mountain stand firm.
—PSALM 30:6–7

With God all things are possible.
—MATTHEW 19:26

If God is for us, who can be against us?
—ROMANS 8:31

Everything is possible for him who believes.
—MARK 9:23

I can do everything through him who gives me strength.
—PHILIPPIANS 4:13

For you have been my hope, O Sovereign LORD,
my confidence since my youth.
—PSALM 71:5

But blessed is the man who trusts in the LORD, whose confidence is in him. He will be like a tree planted by the water that sends out its roots by the stream. It does not fear when heat comes; its leaves are always green. It has no worries in a year of drought and never fails to bear fruit.

—JEREMIAH 17:7–8

I have told you these things, so that in me you may have peace. In this world you will have trouble. But take heart! I have overcome the world.

—JOHN 16:33

Being confident of this, that he who began a good work in you will carry it on to completion until the day of Christ Jesus.

—PHILIPPIANS 1:6

BOOST YOUR OWN WORD POWER

Everywhere you look, people have doubts about themselves. Help them change their minds. Make the most of every contact with every person every day. Who knows what might happen? Someone's lifetime opportunity may be perched on the tip of your tongue. Prompt people with questions. Challenge them with ideas. Fill your own well with God's wisdom, and let him draw from it to water the lives of others. Anticipate the Father's activity. You never know what he will do next! Notice the progress of others and boost them up to the next level of performance. Say something *now*, even if you see only a glimmer of hope. It is likely that when we least expect it, God can use us most. Give the insecure a heaping slice of your own God-confidence. Everyone you meet has a hidden dream or latent destiny. Find out what it is, and do what only you can do to bring it to pass. Speak words of affirmation and encouragement. Back them to the hilt. Remind them of God's faith in them. Let your words ignite the flames of their deepest hopes and desires!

Therefore encourage each other
with these words.

—1 Thessalonians 4:18

AFTER WORDS

As we have seen in these pages, God's pattern is to propel, promote, and provide for his people's destinies through the influence of ordinary individuals. But were these people truly ordinary?

We saw a mother who refused to give up on the salvation of her son, one who prayed and entrusted her child to God for more than thirty years before she saw her reward. This was no ordinary mother.

We learned of a father, who at first glance would have passed for an average Midwest farmer, but the legacy he gave to his son was, in time, felt by hundreds of thousands of people. This was no ordinary father.

And we witnessed teachers, strangers, spouses, and friends who, for no other reason than goodness, seized the simple moments in their grasp and affected the outcomes of millions of lives in the process.

Perhaps these men and women were not so ordinary after all, because they model for us the extraordinary things that can happen when life-giving words are planted in the presence of a hungry, fertile soul.

Each of us arrives here clutching a God-born destiny. And most of our days are spent hurling ourselves at the task of reaching that goal. But how much sweeter, richer, and truly unordinary our lives become when we pause for a moment in the pursuit of our own dreams to help someone else move a bit closer to theirs.

I pray that someday we will open another book and read that you were the spark in someone's life or that one seemingly ordinary day God used your words of support or hope or enthusiasm to inspire yet another of his dreams.

NOTES

CHAPTER 1: CHOICE WORDS OF CHALLENGE

1. Franklin Graham, *Bob Pierce: This One Thing I Do* (Dallas: Word Publishing, 1983).

2. World Vision 1998 Annual Report, World Vision 1999 Web site, http://www.worldvision.org.

3. Charles Colson, *Born Again* (Lincoln, Va.: Chosen Books, Inc., 1976), 112.

4. Jeff Chapman and John D. Jorgenson, eds., *Contemporary Authors*, New Revision Series, vol. 54 (Detroit: Gale Research, 1997), 90.

5. Norman Vincent Peale, *Why Some Positive Thinkers Get Powerful Results* (Nashville: Oliver Nelson Books, 1986), 83.

6. Gay Talese, as cited in *The New York Times*, 28 August 1956, from the Wilson biographies Web site, http://www.wilson-web.com.

7. Ken Blanchard, *We Are the Beloved* (Grand Rapids: Zondervan, 1994).

8. Ken Blanchard Biographical Information, The Ken Blanchard Companies, Escondido, Calif., 1999.

9. Stephen Caldwell, "Gung-ho for God," *Life at Work* 2, no. 6 (n.d.): 61.

10. Ramona Tucker Cramer, "Kay Arthur: A Woman of the Word," *Today's Christian Woman*, May/June 1995, 34.

11. Linda Piepenbrink, "Kay Arthur: Discovering an Awesome God," *Virtue*, October/November 1999, 25.

12. Cramer, "Kay Arthur: A Woman of the Word."

13. Piepenbrink, "Kay Arthur: Discovering an Awesome God," 22.

14. Kay Arthur Biographical Information (Chattanooga, Tenn.: Precept Ministries, 1999).

15. Cramer, "Kay Arthur: A Woman of the Word."

CHAPTER 2: CHOICE WORDS OF CALLING

1. W. Y. Fullerton, *C. H. Spurgeon: A Biography* (Covenant Garden, W.C.2: Williams and Norgate, 1920).

2. Ruth A. Tucker, *From Jerusalem to Irian Jaya* (Grand Rapids: Zondervan, 1983), 70.

3. Jeanne Marie Laskas and Sasha Nyary, "The Good Life and Works of Mister Rogers," *Life*, 1 November 1992, 72.

4. Tom Junod, "Can you say…Hero?" *Esquire*, 1 November 1998, 132.

5. Bill Hybels and Lynne Hybels, *Rediscovering Church* (Grand Rapids: Zondervan, 1995).

6. "The 50 Most Beautiful People: Steve Largent," *People*, 5 May 1996, 88.

7. Jack Friedman and Nick Gallo, "Jocks: Steve Largent Has Caught More Passes than Anyone, but without His Home Team He'd Be Incomplete," *People*, 28 November 1988, 77.

CHAPTER 3: CHOICE WORDS OF COUNSEL

1. John Wooden with Steve Jamison, *Wooden: A Lifetime of Observations and Reflections on and off the Court* (Lincolnwood, Ill.: NTC/Contemporary Publishing, 1997).

2. Rob Reischel, "UW Coach Meets Wooden," *Wisconsin State Journal*, 16 October 1995, 9D.

3. Kenny Moore, "Around the Final Turn of UCLA track," *Sports Illustrated*, 7 May 1993.

4. Wooden with Jamison, *Wooden: A Lifetime of Observations and Reflections*.

5. Robert H. Schuller, *Move Ahead with Possibility Thinking* (New York: Doubleday Dell Publishing Group, 1967).

6. Doug Carroll, "'Hour of Power' Still Going Strong," *Arizona Republic*, 17 October1998, D5.

7. Steve Aveson, "The President's Pastor," Interview with Robert Schuller, ABC *Good Morning America*, 23 March 1997.

8. Crystal Cathedral Web site, 7 January 2000, http://www.crystalcathedral.org/.

9. Lawrence Elliott, *George Washington Carver: The Man Who Overcame* (Englewood Cliffs, N.J.: Prentice-Hall, 1966), 34.

10. John Perry, *Unshakable Faith* (Sisters, Ore.: Multnomah Publishers, 1999).

11. Harry Warfel, *Noah Webster: Schoolmaster to America* (New York: Octagon Books, 1936), 21.

12. Catherine Millard, *Great Statesmen and Heroes* (Camp Hill, Penn.: Horizon Books, 1995), 161.

13. Noah Webster, *An American Dictionary of the English Language* (Springfield, Mass.: George and Charles Merriam, 1828), Preface.

14. Noah Webster, *The Holy Bible, Containing the Old and New Testament in the Common Version* (New Haven, Conn: Durrie & Peck, 1833), Preface.

15. "Noah Webster," *The Columbia Encyclopedia*, 5th ed. (New York: Columbia University Press, 1993), from the Electronic Library, http://www.elibrary.com.

16. Kenneth W. Osbeck, *101 Hymn Stories* (Grand Rapids, Mich.: Kregal Publications, 1982), 181.

17. Ira Sankey, *Sankey's Story of the Gospel Hymns* (Philadelphia: The Sunday School Times Company, 1906), 157.

18. Osbeck, *101 Hymn Stories*, 182.

19. Florence Littauer, telephone interview with author, 14 December 1999.

CHAPTER 4: CHOICE WORDS OF COURAGE

1. Gayle Pollard Terry, "Rosa Parks: Still Fighting for Racial Justice—From the Front of the Bus," *Los Angeles Times*, 19 April 1998, 3.

2. Mark Curnette, "Civil Rights Legend Rosa Parks Being Honored," *Gannett News Service*, 25 October 1998.

3. Sly Jones, "Happy Birthday to You, Rosa Parks," *Minneapolis Star Tribune*, 4 February 1999.

4. Max Lucado, *In the Eye of the Storm* (Dallas: Word Publishing, 1991).

5. Nancy Hellmich, "Max Lucado Suggests Forgiveness," *USA Today*, 4 February 1999, 08(D).

6. "Hold the Fort," Philip P. Bliss, 1870.

7. Sankey, *Sankey's Story of the Gospel Hymns*, 102.

8. Bill Bright, *The Greatest Lesson I've Ever Learned* (San Bernadino, Calif.: Here's Life Publishers, 1990).

CHAPTER 5: CHOICE WORDS OF CORRECTION

1. Betty Lee Skinner, *Daws* (Grand Rapids: Zondervan, 1974), 29.

2. Navigators Web Site Information, http://www.gospelcom.net/navs/.

3. Skinner, *Daws*, 384–85.

4. Kevin Leman, *The Birth Order Book* (Old Tappen, N.J.: Fleming H. Revell Company, 1985).

5. Reggie White, *In the Trenches* (Nashville: Thomas Nelson Publishers, 1996).

6. Tucker, *From Jerusalem to Irian Jaya*, 329.

7. Lyle W. Dorsett, *A Passion for Souls* (Chicago: Moody Press, 1997), 20.

8. Tucker, *From Jerusalem to Irian Jaya*, 331.

9. John Cook, compiler, *The Fairview Guide to Positive Quotations* (Minneapolis: Fairview Press, 1996), 79.

10. Millard Fuller, *Bokotola* (New York: Association Press, 1977), 7.

11. Habitat News, Habitat for Humanity International Web site, December 1999. http://www.habitat.org/newsroom/mth.html.

12. Susan Hogan/Albach, "A Simple Life of Service," *Minneapolis Star Tribune*, 5 July 1997, 5B.

13. Warren Gerard, "Trucker-Turned-Preacher Now Builds Homes for the Needy," *Toronto Star*, 3 April 1999.

CHAPTER 6: CHOICE WORDS OF CONVERSION

1. Mircea Elilade, ed., *The Encyclopedia of Religion* (New York: Macmillan, 1993), 520.

2. F. J. Steed, trans., *Confessions of St. Augustine 1–X* (Kansas City, Mo.: Sneed & Ward, 1942).

3. Elilade, *The Encyclopedia of Religion*, 526.

4. Donald M. Goldstein and Katherine V. Dillon, *God's Samurai: Lead Pilot at Pearl Harbor* (Riverside, N.J.: Macmillian, 1990).

5. Irving McKee, *Ben-Hur Wallace: The Life of General Lew Wallace* (Los Angeles: University of California Press, 1947), 167.

6. Joe Wheeler, *The Man Who Wrote Ben-Hur* (Colorado Springs: Focus on the Family Publishing, 1997), 24.

7. McKee, *Ben-Hur Wallace*, 167.

8. Wheeler, *The Man Who Wrote Ben-Hur*, 27.

9. Author not available, "Magill's Survey of Cinema," 15 June 1995, from the Electronic Library, http://www.elibrary.com.

10. *Ben-Hur the Musical* program, Orlando, Fla., December 1999, 8.

11. Wheeler, *The Man Who Wrote Ben-Hur*, 32.

12. Ronnie Belanger and Brian Mast, eds., *Profiles of Success* (New Brunswick, N.J.: Bridge-Logos Publishers, 1999), 90.

13. Jesusaves.com Web site, http://jabi.com/bookstore/burkett.html.

14. "Amen Corner," *Atlanta Journal and Constitution*, 13 February 1999, G1.

CHAPTER 7: CHOICE WORDS OF CLARITY

1. Pat Williams, *The Magic of Leadership* (Nashville: Thomas Nelson Publishers, 1997), 153.

2. Pat Williams, Biographical Information Sheet, Orlando Magic, Orlando, Fla., November 1999.

3. Pat Williams, Biographical Information Sheet.

4. Linda Piepenbrink, "A Star Is Reborn," *Today's Christian Woman*, July/Aug 1997, 22.

5. Ira J. Hadnot, "Star Power: Ex-Welfare Queen Now Reigns as Critic of the System," *Dallas Morning News*, 3 April 1997, 1C.

6. Piepenbrink, "A Star Is Reborn."

7. Hadnot, "Star Power."

8. John D. Woodbridge, ed., *More than Conquerors* (Chicago: Moody Press, 1992).

9. Emilie Barnes, telephone interview with author, November 1999.

10. Millard, *Great American Statesmen and Heroes*, 172–73.

CHAPTER 8: CHOICE WORDS OF CONCERN

1. Michelle Akers with Judith A. Nelson, *Face to Face with Michelle Akers* (Orlando: Success Factors, 1996).

2. David Smale, "Redirection," *Victory*, June/July 1999, 22.

3. Michelle Akers Web site, http://www.michelleakers.com.

4. Sankey, *Sankey's Story of the Gospel Hymns*, 249.

5. Ibid., 136.

6. Osbeck, *101 Hymn Stories*.

CHAPTER 9: CHOICE WORDS OF COMMERCE

1. Rick Stockton, "Souperman!" *Priorities* 2, no. 3, 33.

2. Andrew Ferguson, Deborah Elder Brown, and Andrea Sachs, "A River of Chicken Soup," *Time*, 8 June 1998, 62.

3. Stockton, "Souperman!"

4. Randee Feldman, Health Communications Inc., e-mail to author, 14 January 2000.

5. Ferguson, Brown, and Sachs, "A River of Chicken Soup."

6. Feldman, e-mail to author, 14 January 2000.

7. Stockton, "Souperman!"

8. Woodbridge, ed., *More Than Conquerors*.

9. Nabisco Company Facts Sheet, Holland, Mich., 1 June 1999.

CHAPTER 10: CHOICE WORDS OF COMPASSION

1. F. W. Boreham, D. D., *The Prodigal* (London, England: Epworth Press, 1941).

2. Matilda Cuomo, *The Person Who Changed My Life* (Syracuse, N.Y.: Carol Publishing Group, 1999), 105.

3. Malcolm Ritter, "Dr. Lorraine Hale—What It Was and Is," *New York Beacon*, 27 March 1995.

4. Yvonne Delaney, "In the Spirit of Mother Hale," *New York Amsterdam News*, 10 June 1999, 9.

5. Vincent F. A. Golphin, "A House of Love," *about...time Magazine*, 31 March 1994.

6. "Hale House Expands Reach," *MedServ Medical News*, 2 October 1999, from the MedServ Web site, http://www.medserv.dk/health/1999/02/10/story08.htm.

7. Golphin, "A House of Love."

8. John D. Woodbridge, ed., *Ambassadors for Christ* (Chicago: Moody Press, 1994).

9. Paul Yonggi Cho, *The Fourth Dimension* (Plainfield, N.J.: Logos International, 1979).

10. Yoido Full Gospel Church Web site, http://www.fgtv.or.kr/n_english/fg_church/yfgc_yoido.afp.

CHAPTER 11: CHOICE WORDS OF CONFIDENCE

1. Og Mandino, *A Better Way to Live*, (New York: Bantam Books, 1990), 41.

2. Maggie Murphy, ed., "News and Notes/Flashes," *Entertainment Weekly*, 16 August 1996.

3. Charles E. Jones, *The People You Meet and the Books You Read* (Harrisburg, Penn.: Executive Books, 1985), Foreword.

4. Stan Smith, interview by the author, 7 December 1999.

5. Stan Smith Biographical Information Sheet, December 1999.

6. Woodbridge, *More Than Conquerors*, 243.

7. John Maxwell and Jim Dornan, *Becoming a Person of Influence* (Nashville: Thomas Nelson Publishers, 1997).

8. Ibid.

9. James Robison, *My Father's Face: A Portrait of the Perfect Father* (Sisters, Ore.: Multnomah Books, 1997).

10. James Robison, interview with the author on *LIFE Today with James Robison*, October 1999.

11. James Robison Biographical Facts Sheet, *LIFE Outreach International*, October 1999.

12. Robison, *My Father's Face*.